~~301.1~~
~~C47t~~   ~~63078~~

DATE DUE			
GAYLORD M-2			PRINTED IN U.S.A.

TWO AGAINST ONE

Coalitions in Triads

THEODORE CAPLOW

Columbia University

Prentice-Hall, Inc., Englewood Cliffs, New Jersey

PRENTICE-HALL SOCIOLOGY SERIES

Neil Smelser, *Series Editor*

© 1968 by Prentice-Hall, Inc., Englewood Cliffs, New Jersey

LIBRARY OF CONGRESS CATALOG CARD NO.: 69-10721

Printed in the United States of America

Current Printing (last digit):
10 9 8 7 6 5 4 3 2 1

PRENTICE-HALL INTERNATIONAL, INC., *London*
PRENTICE-HALL OF AUSTRALIA, PTY. LTD., *Sydney*
PRENTICE-HALL OF CANADA, LTD., *Toronto*
PRENTICE-HALL OF INDIA PRIVATE LTD., *New Delhi*
PRENTICE-HALL OF JAPAN, INC., *Tokyo*

to **C. A. C.**

The Fairest Critic

PREFACE

This volume explores the simple idea that social interaction is essentially triangular rather than linear. "All nature's struggling, associating, and patterning must be based on triangles," says Buckminster Fuller, "because there is no structural validity otherwise." Society is part of nature, and apparently conforms to the same structural principle.

Social interaction, the basic social process whereby persons and groups modify each other's behavior, is triangular—or triadic—because it is always influenced by an audience, present or nearby. The audience interprets the meaning of the interaction, applies customary norms to it, notes what is new or unusual, and incorporates the episode in its own history. Thus the behavior of social actors is monitored on behalf of a larger community.

But the audience to interaction is much more than a Greek chorus, being made up of the friends, relatives, peers, superiors, subordinates, allies, and enemies of the interacting pair. The role of witness can be exchanged at a moment's notice for that of actor, and in the innumerable linked triads that constitute a society there is a constant alternation of active pairs and of dominant coalitions. "From the conversation among three persons that lasts only an hour, to the permanent family of three," wrote Simmel, "there is no triad in which a dissent between any two elements does not occur from time to time . . . and in which the third member does not play a mediating role."

The geometry of triads is full of surprises, for in most triadic situations a coalition of two against one can convert strength into weakness and weakness into strength. In laboratory experiments, coalitions of two weaker subjects against a stronger occur with predictable regularity. In organized social activity, the tendency of the weak to combine against the strong is discouraged by various devices, but the opportunity can never be completely suppressed and the power of a superior is always checked by the threat of coalitions among his subordinates. In the primary triad of father, mother, and child, the formation of a coalition may undermine paternal authority before the child is out of the cradle. In the vast, disorderly milieu of sovereign nations, peace is maintained by a fragile triadic arrangement called a balance of power.

The study of coalitions in triads has scarcely begun, and much more work will be needed before the full possibilities of the subject are discovered. Fortunately, the work is well under way, as evidenced by the recent papers of Bodin, Chertkoff, Stryker, Trost, Vinacke and his associates, Weick and Penner, Willis, Zinnes and many others.

I am grateful to my teachers Clifford Kirkpatrick and Jacques Barzun and to my longtime colleague, the late Arnold M. Rose, for criticism and advice in the early stages of this investigation. Several of my former students, Alfred S. Boote, Edgar Crane, Ronald G. Corwin, Joel Gerstl, Reece J. McGee, and Sheldon Stryker, have undertaken empirical research on coalitions in triads and kindly shared their results with me.

Acknowledgments are due to Professors Morris Freilich, William Gamson, George Peter Murdock, W. Edgar Vinacke, Richard H. Willis, and to the American Sociological Association, the Atherton Press, Basic Books, Inc., The Free Press, the Hogarth Press, Holt, Rinehart & Winston, Inc., The Macmillan Company, Northwestern University Press, and the University of Chicago Press for permission to reproduce copyrighted material in the following pages. Thanks are due also to Bonnie Tocher Green, Addie Sels, and Sally Howlett for patient and careful help with the manuscript.

T. C.

CONTENTS

INTRODUCTION

A *triad* is a social system containing three related members in a persistent situation. It is one of the most familiar phenomena in human experience. Indeed, this essay is an attempt to demonstrate that triads are the building blocks of which all social organizations are constructed.

The members of a triad need not be single persons. They may be three collectivities each acting as a unit. Two triads of the same type may behave very similarly, although one consists of three small boys and the other of three large bureaucracies.

Triads have existed as long as human society and many of their properties were observed long before sociologists existed. The modern discussion of triads was begun by Georg Simmel about 1890, although this discussion did not become animated until the 1950's, when social psychologists began to experiment with triadic situations in the laboratory and to observe triads in real-life settings. What they discovered will be told presently. First, however, let us see why the triad as an object of analysis is distinctive and significant.

PROPERTIES OF TRIADS

Every triad has three members. It is becoming conventional to label them A, B, and C and to designate the most powerful actor A.

1

Every triad contains three relationships: *AB, BC,* and *AC.* The triad is the only social group that has an equal number of members and relationships.

The most significant property of the triad is its tendency to divide into a coalition of two members against the third. The appearance of particular coalitions can be predicted with considerable accuracy if the relative power of the three members be known.

This procedure involves a kind of social geometry, for the occurrence of a coalition cannot be predicted from the previous experience of that particular triad, but must be derived directly from the triadic structure. Consider the following example:

Ahab, Brutus, and Charlie are smugglers who divide their goods on a lonely island far from civil authority. Brutus and Charlie are equally matched. Ahab is slightly more dangerous. He could overpower either Brutus or Charlie in a fight but could easily be overpowered by the two of them together. The situation may be diagrammed as in Figure 1–1.

FIGURE 1–1

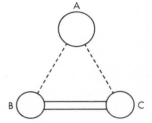

Conditions

• Ahab stronger than Brutus
• Brutus equal to Charlie
• Ahab weaker than others combined

Predicted Outcome
Coalition of Brutus
and Charlie

Ahab will probably try to form a coalition with Brutus or with Charlie, but neither of them would have any reason to accept him as a partner. The predicted coalition is Brutus-Charlie. If Brutus chooses Charlie, he has a partner who does not threaten to dominate him and who needs him for protection against the superior strength and guile of Ahab.

If Brutus were to choose Ahab as a coalition partner, his position would be much less favorable, for he would remain subordinate to Ahab and entirely at his mercy if Charlie were ever removed from the scene. In the Ahab-Brutus coalition a fair division of goods would be much more difficult to work out since contradictory principles seem to apply. Ahab would probably demand the larger share as compensation for the lion's share he would have obtained in the absence of a coalition. Brutus would probably be unwilling to accept a lesser share since Ahab could not form a winning coalition alone, and their contributions are equal in that sense. Brutus might even demand a premium for his risk in accepting Ahab as a partner. Whatever compromise they reach is likely to be less acceptable to one than to the other and therefore unstable.

We do not anticipate that a *BC* coalition would be formed in every situation of this type, but a strain towards its formation will probably be felt, and in a random sample of similar situations, the *BC* coalition should appear very frequently. Even when no coalition is formed, or the "wrong" coalitions appear, some pressure towards the formation of the predicted coalition will probably be experienced by the participants and will affect the outcome of the situation.

The foregoing example illustrates the most distinctive feature of triadic social systems: the transformation of strength into weakness and weakness into strength. The margin of superiority Ahab enjoys as he lands on the island insures his defeat. If he could divest himself of this superiority, becoming equal to Brutus and Charlie, his chances of joining a winning coalition would then be 2 to 1, since all coalitions are equally likely in egalitarian triads. (See Figure 1–2.)

FIGURE 1–2

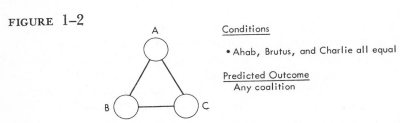

Conditions

• Ahab, Brutus, and Charlie all equal

Predicted Outcome
Any coalition

More surprising still, if Ahab's loss of strength were to continue until he became much weaker than Brutus or Charlie, he might be certain of a good share of the spoils; his present weakness is clearly advantageous, just as his strength would have formerly been a handicap. The situation would be as shown in Figure 1–3.

The greatly diminished and enfeebled Ahab is now sought out as a coalition partner by both Brutus and Charlie and, within reason, he can make his own terms with one of them. The causes of this new popularity are self-evident, neatly reversing the reasons he was avoided in his more powerful days. Both Brutus and Charlie, now giants to his pygmy eyes, are enthusiastic about a coalition partner whom they can readily dominate and with whose help they can subdue an otherwise equal adversary. The offers Ahab would receive from them might reach an equal share or even more.

In this last variation of the example, Ahab becomes what Simmel called the *"tertius gaudens,"* the "enjoying third." He holds the key to the situation because his lesser strength can tip the balance in favor of either one of his more powerful friends.

Further implications of this mechanism will occupy us throughout this

FIGURE 1–3

Conditions

- Ahab weaker than Brutus
- Brutus equal to Charlie
- Brutus and Charlie each
  seeking a coalition
  with Ahab

Predicted Outcome
   A coalition of Ahab
   and Brutus, or Ahab
   and Charlie

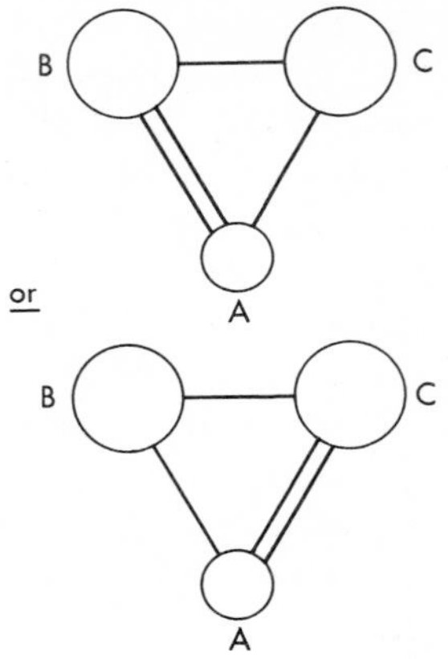

or

book. The transformation of strength to weakness and of weakness to strength in the triad helps to explain the balance struck between the rulers and the ruled in every human society. Unlimited oppression is only possible when rulers and ruled do not belong to the same social system. Whenever they are linked by interaction in an organizational matrix, the triadic mechanism works its multiple transformations up and down the status scale so that the will of the master is always subject at some points to that of the servant. The checks administered by the weak to the strong are unintentional, so to speak, but they cannot be parried or avoided without tearing apart the whole web of social dependence from which authority is derived.

Triads have other interesting properties. For example, they exhibit catalytic effects. Each of the pair relationships in a triad may occur alone or in the presence of the third member. His presence, however passive, always modifies the relationship of the other two. The simpler catalytic effects follow sociological principles that we first discover for ourselves in nursery school—the presence of an antagonist increases one's affection for a friend and the presence of a friend increases one's hostility towards a common antagonist. Thus, in a triad containing a *BC* coalition, the presence of *A* tends to reinforce the solidarity of *B* and *C* and encourages them to make gestures of mutual esteem. Simultaneously, the antagonism between *A* and *B* is sharpened by the presence of *C*, while *A* and *C* are further estranged by mere proximity to *B*. A long-established triad with an accumulation of complex sentiments may show quite different relationships in each of its pairs, depending on the presence or absence of the third member.

Another type of catalytic effect modifies organizational status. Much of the world's work is accomplished by hierarchical triads such as leader-lieutenant-follower, master-journeyman-apprentice, or manager-foreman-worker. Each of these has a man in the middle who bears the brunt of the tension between discipline and freedom by sustaining nearly incompatible relationships with his superior and his subordinate. In general, the presence of a person who witnesses the interaction of a pair of unequals tends to increase their inequality, and his departure reduces the status difference. Thus, the foreman is much closer to the manager and much more managerial in his orientation when the worker is absent. When he is alone with the worker he is less authoritarian and may choose to identify himself as a worker with a worker's grievances. When the three men are together the pressure on the foreman to play incompatible roles is sometimes intolerable.

It is possible to describe any complex status order as a set of overlapping hierarchical triads. When and how it is useful to do so will be shown in later chapters.

THE EIGHT TYPES OF TRIADS

Several types of triads, differing in power distribution, were mentioned in the previous section. Taking power into account, there are eight basic types, as shown in Figure 1–4.

This classification of triads is useful for many purposes. In most of the experimental games that have been played with triads in the laboratory, the power distribution has been represented by weights assigned to each player. In observational studies of "real" triads, the power distribution reflects relative influence. In organizational studies, the *expected* power distribution is expressed by the formal statuses of the three actors. In triads whose members are collectivities, the power distribution can often be measured by counting the number of soldiers, votes, or dollars controlled by each member.

Note, however, that the power distribution gives us only a partial description of a triad. Even the most simplified analysis must take into account the different *situations* in which the triad may appear:

Continuous Situations. The members of the triad are permanently related to each other within a larger social system which requires them to interact. The triad is a cog in the larger system's machinery. Coalitions are formed for a variety of purposes, but the triad is expected to maintain some degree of unity despite its internal divisions. Although one coalition may be dominant most of the time, the two other coalitions are expected to form when appropriate. The history of such a triad is a long sequence of revocable choices.

Episodic Situations. The triad is again located within a permanent

FIGURE 1–4

The Eight Types of Triads [1]

Type 1

A = B = C

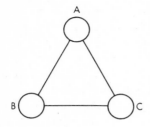

Type 2

A > B
B = C
A < (B+C)

Type 3

A < B
B = C

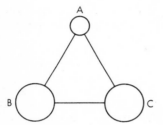

Type 4

A > (B+C)
B = C

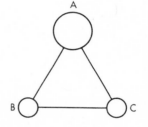

Type 5

A > B > C
A < (B+C)

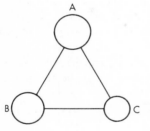

Type 6

A > B > C
A > (B+C)

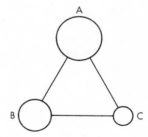

Type 7

A > B > C
A = (B+C)

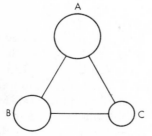

Type 8

A = (B+C)
B = C

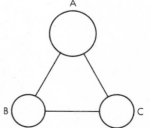

[1] As originally presented in "Further Development of a Theory of Coalitions in the Triad," *American Journal of Sociology*, **XLIV** (March 1959), 488.

organization, but the object of a coalition is to secure an advantage in a contest governed by explicit rules. In a legislature, for example, the episodes are votes on bills, which are preceded by extensive maneuvering towards the formation of a winning coalition. The coalition dissolves as soon as the vote has been taken, although each episode has some influence on subsequent events. This particular case—the formation of legislative coalitions—has been well studied, and some interesting hypotheses about it have been developed, for example, that the minimum winning coalition is the one most likely to be formed.

Terminal Situations. In a terminal situation the triad exists unwillingly, so to speak. Like Ahab, Brutus, and Charlie, the members of such triads would prefer to be alone and each looks for opportunities to get rid of his fellows. Coalitions are formed for both aggressive and defensive motives, for profit and for protection, to destroy the opponent or to prevent further realignments. Sovereign nations poised in a massive balance of power exemplify this situation.

Continuous, episodic, and terminal situations must be separately studied because they lead to different outcomes when coalitions are formed. Consider the classic case of the Type 5 triad diagrammed in Figure 1–5. In the continuous situation we anticipate a BC or AC coalition. Before the formation of a coalition, C is dominated by both A and B and therefore seeks a coalition partner. B is receptive to C's invitation; since if a BC coalition is formed, B will dominate A by virtue of the coalition, instead of being dominated by A, and B will continue to dominate C within the coalition. He has nothing to gain from an AB coalition, which may therefore be ruled out. Faced with the threat of a BC coalition, A may advance counteroffers to C, to whom he is an attractive partner, provided that C is indifferent to the margin by which he is overmatched within the winning coalition.

In the episodic situation each member of the triad seeks a position of advantage with respect to each distribution of reward. A larger share of reward is preferred to a smaller share, but any share is preferred to none. Given a Type 5 triad, the necessity of entering a coalition in order to win is self-evident. The realization that any actor wins by entering any coalition and loses by staying out will suggest an *equal* distribution of the reward, while the unequal contributions of the coalition members to the margin of victory will suggest an *unequal* distribution. Although these two principles cannot be completely reconciled, the strain can be reduced by choosing the minimum winning coalition BC. In legislative episodes that conform to the model this does appear to be the usual outcome.[2]

2 William H. Riker, *The Theory of Political Coalitions* (New Haven: Yale University Press, 1962).

FIGURE 1–5

Anticipated Coalitions in a Type 5 Triad

In a continuous situation

A > B > C
A < (B+C)

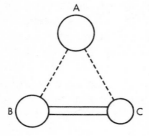 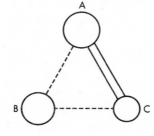

a <u>BC</u> or <u>AC</u>
coalition

In an episodic situation

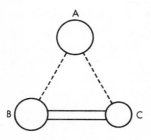

a <u>BC</u> coalition

In a terminal situation

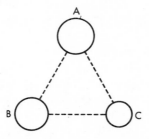

no coalition

In the terminal situation any coalition is directed towards a single redistribution of power which dissolves the triad or changes its power distribution beyond recognition. Under terminal conditions no coalition is likely to be formed in the Type 5 triad since every possible coalition would have a weaker member who would be helpless after the opponent had been disposed of. A *BC* coalition to partition *A* would have to award *C* a disproportionate share of the spoils to make him equal to *B*. Other-

wise, the partition of *A* would leave *B* free to destroy *C*. It is most unlikely that *B* would agree to any division of spoils whereby the weaker *C*
would receive the lion's share. At most, *B* might concede an equal division,
which *C* would find to be insufficient protection.

This is a crude model of a "balance of power." It may be quite stable
if potential conflicts are limited to a single triad, as was the case in the
first twenty years of the nuclear age, with the United States as *A,* the
Soviet Union as *B,* and the rest of the world as *C*. It becomes very precarious when the coalition possibilities are too complex to be fully predictable.

A NOTE ON DYADS, TETRADS, PENTADS, ETC.

The assertion that a social group with three members is qualitatively
different from a group of any other size has overtones of mysticism
hardly consonant with sociological rationality. Let us examine the
rationale for this assertion.

A dyad cannot ordinarily constitute an organization because it has no
collective identity apart from its two principals. Replacing one of a
couple creates a new couple, not a continuation of the old one, except
under highly unusual circumstances.[3] But it takes no more than three
members to establish a collective identity capable of surviving the replacement of one member by another.

The matter may be viewed in another way. In a brilliant essay Nadel
points out that the interaction of any pair of complementary roles in an
institutional system is generally witnessed by related third parties.[4] These
witnesses have a personal stake in the outcome of the interactions which
they observe (for example, a parent is legitimately concerned with the
relationships between his children). Such witnesses may be said to
monitor relationships on behalf of the larger social system, maintaining
a link between social norms and private relationships.

A similar model of interaction—involving two combatants and a
witness—is applicable to organized conflict. A *mêlée* is unstable regardless
of the scale of the conflict. The impulse to form coalitions with others
who are fighting the same enemy is strategically irresistible and will
usually continue until all of the active combatants have been polarized
into two camps. At some stage most conflicts can be diagrammed as a
triad composed of a pair of combatants and an uncommitted witness to
whom each of the combatants appeals for support. The outcome of the

---

3 For example, when each participant holds multiple positions. Any play might con-
ceivably be performed by two actors since only one or two voices are heard at the same
time, but it strains the imagination to describe a pair of actors as a theatrical company.

4 S. F. Nadel, *The Theory of Social Structure* (New York: Free Press of Glencoe,
Inc., 1964).

conflict is often decided by the formation of a coalition between one of the combatants and the witness. There is also the possibility of a surprise coalition by the combatants against the witness.

All of these processes, of course, can be observed in tetrads, pentads, and higher-numbered groups. Willis has shown that a theory of coalitions in the triad can be extended to tetrads with only a few additional assumptions, although with a considerable increase of complexity.[5] There is no apparent reason why the coalitions in an octad could not be predicted by a computer if the initial power distribution and the rules of the situation were known. But such a scheme would be impossible to visualize and impracticable to verify. For the time being it is more convenient to reduce larger groups to triadic form by combining like-acting members. The elucidation of social processes in the triad is sufficiently challenging in itself.

A DESCRIPTION OF THE CHAPTERS TO FOLLOW

Chapter II, "In Praise of Georg Simmel," will return to the starting point of sociological inquiry into triads and review Simmel's deceptively simple observations on the nature of interaction in groups of three.

Chapter III, "Around the Pachisi Board," retraces a line of investigation followed by experimental social psychologists for more than a decade. Many experiments with laboratory triads have used an experimental pachisi game to examine the formation of coalitions in triads. The results seem to confirm the expectation that coalitions can be predicted from power distributions although there have been a few anomalous findings and some unexpected discoveries.

Chapter IV, "Apish Tricks," briefly reports certain aspects of the behavior of apes and monkeys, as observed in their natural surroundings by patient and courageous zoologists. It seems to be well-established that these primates, poised on the borderline between animal and human awareness, establish triads and form coalitions in them.

Chapter V, "Organizational Triads," is an expansion of my previous papers on the theory of coalitions in triads, with special reference to triads in organizations. The restated theory still attempts to predict coalitions from initial power distributions, but takes account of other factors as well.

Chapter VI, "The Primary Triad," discusses in some detail the formation of coalitions in triads composed of father, mother, and child.

Chapter VII, "Other Family Triads," considers several kinship constellations that are socially and emotionally significant in nearly every known

[5] Richard H. Willis, "Coalitions in the Tetrad," *Sociometry*, XXV, No. 4 (December 1962), pp. 358–76.

society: grandparent-parent-child, sibling triads, husband-wife-mother-in-law, and father-son-uncle.

Chapter VIII, "The Motives of Hamlet," applies triad theory to the best known work of English literature to see whether our understanding of either the play or the theory is thereby increased.

Chapter IX, "Full-Fledged Games," examines the process of coalition formation in large organizations in which many different interests are pursued. The cases discussed are based on empirical studies carried out in diverse settings: a state-owned industrial enterprise, an advertising agency, and a community controversy.

Chapter X, "The March of History," deals with triads of a much larger scale, whose members are parties, classes, and nations. Triadic models for war and revolution are developed and some connections between them are traced.

IN PRAISE
OF GEORG SIMMEL

Georg Simmel (1858–1918) taught at the Universities of Berlin and Strasbourg and is recognized as one of the principal founders of modern sociology. He and his contemporary, Emile Durkheim, are often described as co-founders, although in some textbooks they must share this honor with Max Weber, Vilfredo Pareto, and Lester F. Ward.

Simmel was a cultivated man, thoughtful, detached, and worldly. He wrote on Italian architecture, lectured on German poetry, concerned himself with modern painting, women's fashions and the history of pantheism. Some of his essays, such as "The Ruin" and "The Handle," are existentialist in subject and style. Unlike Durkheim, who devoted his life to the skillful exposition of a single fundamental idea, and unlike Weber, the scholarly specialist, Simmel moved in the main current of European thought. The intellectual problems that interested him ranged beyond sociology: freedom and free will, the metaphysics of death, and the psychological effects of metropolitan life. No subject was too large or too small for his consideration if it had a theoretical character. His papers on "How Is Society Possible?" and on the meaning of history were interspersed with essays on the philosophy of chess and the principles of portrait painting.

For a founding father, Simmel seems curiously remote from organized sociology, and for almost fifty years it has been customary to deplore the neglect into which he has fallen. In his lifetime he had difficulties with the academic establishment. Durkheim and Weber criticized his work somewhat irritably, and Dilthey is said to have blocked his promotion to a permanent chair at Berlin.[1] The two principal texts that introduced American students of succeeding generations to European sociology, Pitirim Sorokin's *Contemporary Sociological Theories* and Talcott Parsons' *Structure of Social Action,* barely mention him.

However, the neglect of Simmel is less striking than the efforts of a crowd of scholars to remedy it. His books and papers were read earlier and more widely than those of Durkheim and Weber. Albion Small, the organizing genius of American sociology, translated Simmel for the *American Journal of Sociology* in 1896, and continued to do so for fifteen years. Simmel was a leading spirit in the first international association of sociologists; and Gassen's bibliography of significant writings about him, compiled in 1959, filled eighteen pages [2] (it would be much longer if brought up to date). His enthusiastic disciples are now more numerous than ever.

The impression of neglect may stem from a discrepancy between Simmel's style of thought and the prevailing sociological idiom. Following Durkheim's example, sociology began to rely increasingly on statistical data obtained by empirical research. And following Weber's, it framed its discourse more and more in a language of special terms and concepts, either invented for the purpose of sociological analysis or modified from their common meanings. These new ways of writing and thinking about social systems can only be used by professionals.

Simmel, for all his learning, cultivated the attitudes of a dilettante, as much at home in philosophy, history, psychology, esthetics, and literary criticism as in formal sociology. He must have had a constitutional aversion to statistical measurement. So far as I know, he never used quantitative data for any purpose, not even in an anecdote. He seems to have envisioned sociological progress to be an increase of understanding by the sheer power of ratiocination and not to have attached any importance to the accumulation of descriptive facts.

Indeed, although Simmel discussed the scientific future of sociology at length and was probably the first to circumscribe a manageable subject matter for it, he conceived of the discipline in a different way than most contemporary sociologists, who want to describe the human sector of the

---

[1] He was also rejected for a chair at Heidelberg; an extraordinarily nasty evaluation of him submitted on that occasion by a Berlin colleague has been published in Lewis Coser, ed., *Georg Simmel* (Englewood Cliffs, N.J.: Prentice-Hall, Inc., 1965), pp. 37–39.

[2] Kurt Gassen, "Bibliography of Writings about Georg Simmel," in Kurt H. Wolff, trans. and ed., *Georg Simmel, 1858–1918* (Columbus: Ohio State University Press, 1959).

universe as accurately as possible, uncovering hidden regularities for science's sake, or to enlarge man's control over the environment. Simmel's curiosity had a different character altogether. He studied sociology, as he studied metaphysics, in order to come to terms with reality, to master his own fate by grasping the rules of the game of existence. Knowledge achieved in this way might guide other men towards the good life or fortify their courage by dispelling some of the mystery that surrounds experience, but any benefits that accrued to social planning would be quite fortuitous.

It is paradoxical, therefore, that modern empirical sociology, with its quantitative and technical bias, owes so much to Simmel. His powerful intellect confronted the fundamentals of individual and collective experience and evolved new modes of thinking about experience whose possibilities have still not been fully appraised. Triad theory is an example of an "area" discovered and so grandly surveyed by Simmel that each new increment of information from empirical research raises problems already identified and half-resolved in his essays.

Nevertheless, the difference of purpose between Simmel and present-day sociologists is too great to permit easy translation. He would probably have regarded the contemporary use of his ideas in laboratory experiments as utterly absurd, perpetually losing the point of his distinctions in pseudo-technical statements. To the modern experimenter, Simmel is an exasperating grandfather, too far removed from practical life to impart the wisdom he possesses. In the remainder of this chapter we shall try to present Simmel's triad theory in a language situated approximately between his and ours, preserving as much as possible of his almost superhuman insight, but adapting it freely to our own purposes.

The problem of sociology, Simmel wrote, ". . . is the identification, systematic arrangement, psychological explanation, and historical development of the pure forms of socialization." [3] His major contribution to the study of the pure forms of socialization was the identification of an essential dualism in all social experience. He viewed any social structure as a balance of positive and negative forces, centrifugal and centripetal tendencies. Simmel was an anti-utopian, for whom evil is not an interference with the orderly workings of good, but its counterbalance:

> . . . social unity is not the result merely of harmonious tendencies and integrating forces, but the differentiating tendencies play also a positive role. Just as the cosmos needs love and hatred, attractive and repulsive forces to obtain form, so also society needs a certain quantitative relation of harmony

[3] Nicholas J. Spykman, *The Social Theory of Georg Simmel,* adaptations from works of Georg Simmel (New York: Atherton Press, 1966), p. 40.

and disharmony, association and competition, friendship and jealousy, to obtain a definite structure.[4]

Simmel's dialectic is at least as consistent as Hegel's and pervades all of his thinking about social experience. Any social situation may be resolved into positive and negative tendencies *plus* their synthesis, and it is the synthesis—the reconciliation of opposing tendencies—that constitutes the core of the situation. Man is partly individual and partly social, desires both autonomy and the security of the crowd, wants to obey authority and to resist it, craves both submission and domination.

> His existence, if we analyze its contents, is not only partly social and partly individual, but also belongs to the fundamental, decisive, and irreducible category of a unity which we cannot designate other than as the synthesis or simultaneity of two logically contradictory characterizations of man—the characterization which is based on his function as a member, as a product and a content of society; and the opposing characterization which is based on his functions as an autonomous being, and which views his life from its own center and for its own sake.[5]

The demands of any social system on its individual members are necessarily excessive. The system claims from the individual a total commitment which he is unwilling to give, and the individual, on his own behalf, seeks more freedom, comfort, and support from the system than it is ever willing to grant him. Organizational programs are never carried out exactly as planned because they always and necessarily collide with the private programs of individuals.

> Society asks of the individual that he employ all his strength in the service of the special function which he has to exercise as a member of it; that he so modify himself as to become the most suitable vehicle for this function. Yet the drive toward unity and wholeness that is characteristic of the individual himself rebels against this role. . . . This conflict between the whole, which imposes the one-sidedness of partial function upon its elements, and the part, which itself strives to be a whole, is insoluble.[6]

The insoluble conflict between the individual and society is waged internally as well as externally. Human nature itself is composed of both social and nonsocial elements. Inner consciousness—what Simmel calls "ethical substance"—is affected by two incompatible virtues: conformity to the collective will and defiance of it. Hence, the biography of the serious man is necessarily tragic.

4 *Ibid.*, p. 29.

5 Georg Simmel, "How Is Society Possible?" in Wolff, trans. and ed., *op. cit.*, pp. 350–51.

6 Georg Simmel, *The Sociology of Georg Simmel*, Kurt H. Wolff, trans., ed., and introd. (New York: Free Press of Glencoe, Inc., 1950), p. 59.

Simmel's theory of conflict was originally derived from Immanuel Kant's *Principles and Politics,* especially from Kant's notion that Nature ingeniously set men at odds with each other so that law and civilization might emerge from the necessity of controlling their antagonisms. But Simmel's conception is more subtle. He believed that conflict contributes to the development of social structure in several ways:

Aggregates of individuals are welded into groups by the appearance of a common enemy. The enemy need not be fierce. A mere outsider or stranger has this effect.

The boundary lines between groups in conflict become an organizational framework. Boundary maintenance underlies all other collective activities.

Conflict is itself a form of interaction involving communication, reciprocal influence, and the development of a new unity, sometimes at the cost of destroying the original parties. Conflict leads inevitably to settlement, which is a special form of synthesis. Differences in power are both causes and consequences of conflict.

This last point deserves amplification. Simmel was the first sociologist to grasp the significance of what is now called status (he called it submission) in describing a social system or understanding the events that take place within it. "The most important form of relationship in the whole social world," he wrote, "is the relationship between the leader and his followers, between the superior and his subordinates. It is a form of socialization without which no social life would be possible, and the main factor sustaining the unity of groups." [7]

The status relationship has its roots in both conflict and cooperation. Inequality is not acknowledged without a struggle, but it involves an element of reciprocity. Submission to authority is never passive and the subordinate always has some measure of control over the superior. Authority arises from transactions that involve the spontaneous and active participation of subordinates, which is elicited in various ways—sometimes by personal faith and confidence, more often by the transfer of dignity to the superior from a large organization to which the subordinates have already pledged their allegiance. Whatever the circumstances, conflict continues to figure in every status relationship in two ways: first, the willingness of subordinates to accept authority is greatly enhanced by the presence of a common enemy who threatens the boundaries of the group; and second, the subordinates of a single superior may be counted on to develop solidarity among themselves in order to resist their common ruler and adversary. The universality of conflict accounts for the appearance of status orders in all organizations and also explains

---

[7] Spykman, *op. cit.,* p. 95.

the internal dissension by which all organizations are weakened and eventually undermined.

The universality of conflict and cooperation—conflict tempered by cooperation, cooperation limited by conflict—also underlies Simmel's geometrical model of interaction. Long before Kurt Lewin proposed the *life space* as a basic concept for social psychology, Simmel regarded the description of interaction in spatial terms as a kind of inescapable metaphor:

> Interaction between human beings is conceived of and experienced as space-filling. If individuals live within certain spatial boundaries and are isolated from one another, the space between them is empty space. But if they enter into reciprocal relations, the space between them seems filled and animated.[8]

From this it is only a short step to recognition of the "boundary line" that appears between individuals in contact, around contiguous groups, and wherever else a conflict is contemplated or possible. The boundary line shows what provocation will cause a battle and where the battle-ground will be:

> The existence of a sociological boundary line between groups of individuals means the existence of a special form of interaction for which we have no single term. It means a relationship which contains in a latent form an attitude of both defense and offense. It may be a line delimiting the rights of the individuals at the end of a struggle, or a line indicating the delimiting of their respective influence preceding a struggle.[9]

The spatial representation of sociological relationships and the identification of every group boundary as the locus of a potential conflict set the scene for Simmel's penetrating analysis of interaction in triads.

It should be noted that Simmel never spoke of *dyads* or *triads,* but used a variety of expressions for groups of two and three, especially *zweierverbindung* and *dreiverbindung.* Albion Small, in his translations of Simmel's papers for the early volumes of the *American Journal of Sociology,* introduced *dyad* and *triad,* as well as *monad* and *tetrad.* They have been used by all later translators and since the appearance of the *Systematic Sociology* of von Wiese and Becker [10] in 1932, by most writers. As is so often the case, the translated term has overtones that were not present in the original. The word *triad* suggests a closer, more integrated, and more harmonious relationship than *zweierverbindung;* it is also more structural. Simmel's discussion is explicitly concerned with patterns

8 *Ibid.,* p. 145.
9 *Ibid.,* p. 148.
10 Leopold von Wiese and Howard Becker, *Systematic Sociology* (New York: John Wiley & Sons, Inc., 1932).

of social relationships involving three elements, whereas modern triad theory deals with three-member groups. This is in part attributable to progression from general reflections to the analysis of particular cases, but it also involves a shift of meaning, similar to that which occurred when Simmel's *Die Kreuzung socialer Kreise* was translated as *The Web of Group Affiliations*.[11]

It is noteworthy that Simmel never discussed coalitions directly. The impression that he did is difficult to dispel, but his discussion of triads focused on the role of the third party added to an existing dyad, and he gave little attention to the choice between coalition partners, which figures as the central problem of recent studies.

He begins by differentiating the dyad from all larger groups:

> . . . the difference between the dyad and larger groups consists in the fact that the dyad has a different relation to each of its two elements than have larger groups to *their* members. Although, for the outsider, the group consisting of two may function as an autonomous, super-individual unit, it usually does not do so for its participants. Rather, each of the two feels himself confronted only by the other, not by a collectivity above him. The social structure here rests immediately on the one and on the other of the two, and the secession of either would destroy the whole. The dyad, therefore, does not attain that super-personal life which the individual feels to be independent of himself. As soon, however, as there is a sociation of three, a group continues to exist even in case one of the members drops out.[12]

He goes on to say that dyads, like their two members, are certain of their own mortality, whereas triads and larger groups are potentially immortal since their members can be replaced one by one. This subtle difference colors all of the attitudes that develop around dyads and larger groups.

In another famous passage he introduces the distinction between direct and indirect relationships and the tendency of triads to divide into a pair and an intruder:

> Where three elements, *A, B, C,* constitute a community, there is added to the immediate relationship which exists, for example, between *A* and *B*, the immediate relationship which they gain by their common relation to *C*. This is unquestionably a sociological enrichment, apart from the bond by the straight and shortest line; each pair of elements are now joined by a broken line. Points upon which the pair could find no immediate contact are put in reciprocal relationship by the third element, which offers to each another side, and joins these, nevertheless, in the unity of its personality. Separations which the parties could not of themselves reconcile are accommodated by the

11 Georg Simmel, *Conflict*, Kurt H. Wolff, trans., and *The Web of Group Affiliations,* Reinhard Bendix, trans. (New York: Free Press of Glencoe, Inc., 1955).
12 Simmel, *The Sociology of Georg Simmel, op. cit.*, p. 123.

In Praise of Georg Simmel

third, or by their being included in a comprehensive whole. On the other hand, the direct union is not merely strengthened by the indirect, but it may also be destroyed. There is no relationship so complete between three that each individual may not, under certain circumstances, be regarded by the other two as an intruder, even if it is only to the extent of [not] sharing in certain moods. . . .[13]

The significance of the differentiation between dyads and triads, according to Simmel, is much sharper than between triads and tetrads or higher-numbered groups. Indeed, triads and higher-numbered groups can be reduced to triadic form. The change from a childless marriage to a family with a single child is a dramatic one. Succeeding children have less effect, partly because the family has acquired, once and for all, the "super-personal" character of triads and larger groups, partly because triads may have collective members. For example, the second child may be added as a third member to a dyadic relationship between the parents acting as a unit and the first child. Or the two children may act as a unit in a triad whose two other actors are their parents.

In this connection, Simmel carefully points out that the structure of a status relationship changes when there are two subordinates instead of one.[14] A single servant will approach and identify himself with his employer "from the natural need of attachment" but two servants will "compose a party" against their employer based on the same need and on the similarity of their situations. He remarks that it is easier for a superior to keep two subordinates than one at a distance and to obtain their compliance, introducing without fuss or bother the important principle of the catalytic influence of a third party on the relationship between unequals.

Simmel distinguished three functions for the third party in a triad and explored the varieties of each function with the aid of historical examples. Although he uses the dyad as the point of departure and considers the third party only in relation to the pair, he is fully aware that the real triad in a continuous situation is involved in a game of musical chairs:

From the conversation among three persons that lasts only an hour, to the permanent family of three, there is no triad in which a dissent between any two elements does not occur from time to time—a dissent of a more harmless or more pointed, more momentary or more lasting, more theoretical or more practical nature—and in which the third member does not play a mediating role. . . . This function makes the round among the three elements, since

[13] Georg Simmel, "The Number of Members as Determining the Sociological Form of the Group," *American Journal of Sociology,* VIII, No. 1 (July 1902), 45–46.
[14] *Ibid.,* p. 162.

the ebb and flow of social life realizes the form of conflict in every possible combination of two members.[15]

The possible functions of the "third member" as described by Simmel are: (1) as mediator, (2) as *tertius gaudens,* and (3) as oppressor.

The mediator stands between contending parties and hinders them from engaging in conflict. He can accomplish this because he is non-partisan. He may be nonpartisan because he stands above the opposing interests and is indifferent to the outcome or because he is closely involved with both sides and cannot be indifferent. The mediator tries to preserve the continuity of the group on occasions when the contestants are willing to shatter it in order to overpower each other. No matter how he is chosen for his role, he becomes the group's representative, defending the collective program against private interests.

The appearance of a mediator in a triad signals the absence of a coalition, for the two contestants are incapable of forming a coalition because of their opposing interests, and the mediator guarantees not to be party to a coalition by announcing his impartiality.

The *tertius gaudens,* the "enjoying third," turns the dissension of the two other parties to his own advantage and sacrifices the interests of the group to his private program. The general form of the relationship is that both contestants bid for his support so that he is able to obtain an exploitative price for it. In terms of coalition theory the *tertius gaudens* is the partner wanted by both other members of a triad when they have conclusively rejected each other.

The oppressor follows a policy of instigating conflict between the other two parties for his own purposes. Sometimes he does this in subtle and ingenious ways, like the Inca prince who divided newly conquered tribes almost in half and placed a chief over each part with just enough disparity in rank to assure a quarrel. In other instances the oppressor is a passive beneficiary, profiting from the mutual contention of the other two to take liberties they would not ordinarily permit.

The oppressor is always aware of potential coalitions, and his tactics are designed to prevent the formation of a coalition against himself. Although he dominates the situation, his position is precarious compared to that of a high-status mediator, who can watch the formation of a coalition between the other two members of the triad with benign approval.

---

[15] Simmel, *The Sociology of Georg Simmel, op. cit.,* pp. 148–49.

AROUND THE
PACHISI BOARD

Pachisi [1] is a very ancient board game resembling backgammon. Each player has a marker, whose moves are determined by a throw of dice. In the simplest form of the game the player throws a pair of dice when his turn comes and moves his marker a number of squares equal to the number he has thrown. The squares are arranged in a path, and the goal is at the end of the path, so that the player whose marker arrives first at the end of the path wins. Infinite elaboration is possible in the game and there are many variant forms such as *Monopoly* and *Careers*. Pachisi has been very useful in the socio-psychological laboratory.

THE VINACKE-ARKOFF GAME

In 1956, Vinacke and Arkoff at the University of Hawaii devised a form of pachisi for the study of coalitions in the triad. [2] It is an unusually simple form: there are three players; the board has a single path of sixty-seven spaces numbered consecutively; before a game each player draws a tab which assigns him a

---

[1] The correct spelling, from the Hindu *Pachisi. Parcheesi* is a trademark and *Parchesi* is incorrect.

[2] W. Edgar Vinacke and Abe Arkoff, "An Experimental Study of Coalitions in the Triad," *American Sociological Review*, XXII, No. 4 (August 1957), 406–14.

weight for that game; a single die is thrown instead of a pair; and at each move the player advances his marker a number of spaces equal to the number thrown times his assigned weight.

The game is an instrument for studying the effect of an initial power distribution on the formation of coalitions in triads. The weight drawn by a player represents his power for that game and the weights drawn by all three players are a power distribution.

The Vinacke-Arkoff game is unusual in that every player moves on every throw of the die. In most forms of pachisi each player moves his marker only on his own throw, and the outcome of the game is determined by chance, although there is some opportunity for skill or strategy. Under the Vinacke-Arkoff rules the outcome of a game would be obvious as soon as the weights were drawn if the players were not allowed to form coalitions and, in fact, the outcome is fully determined as soon as a coalition has been formed or the players have decided to proceed without one. As most players learned, the game need never be played to the end.

Each group of subjects played eighteen games, repeating six power distributions in random sequence. How they were seated is not known, but it seems likely from the results that they sat along one side of a table.

The predictions to be tested in this experiment were drawn from a paper I had published a few months earlier which suggested that under certain conditions the formation of particular coalitions depends upon the initial distribution of power in the triad and may be predicted to some extent when the initial distribution of power is known.[3] The conditions specified were that: (1) members of a triad may differ in strength, (2) a stronger member can control a weaker member and will seek to do so, (3) each member of the triad seeks control over the others, preferring control over two others to control over one, (4) strength is additive, and (5) the strength of a coalition is equal to the sum of the initial strengths of its members. The detailed predictions were as follows (and as shown in Figure 3–1).

Type 1.   In this simplest case, all three members are of equal strength. This is the classic, but probably not the most common, type of triad. The coalitions *AB*, *BC,* and *AC* are equally likely, and each member strives to enter a coalition within which he will be equal to his ally and stronger (by virtue of the coalition) than the isolate.

Type 2.   One member is stronger than the other two, but not much stronger. Again, all three members seek a coalition, since to be isolated

[3] "A Theory of Coalitions in the Triad," *American Sociological Review,* XXI, No. 4 (August 1956), 489–93.

FIGURE 3-1

The Vinacke-Arkoff Game [4]

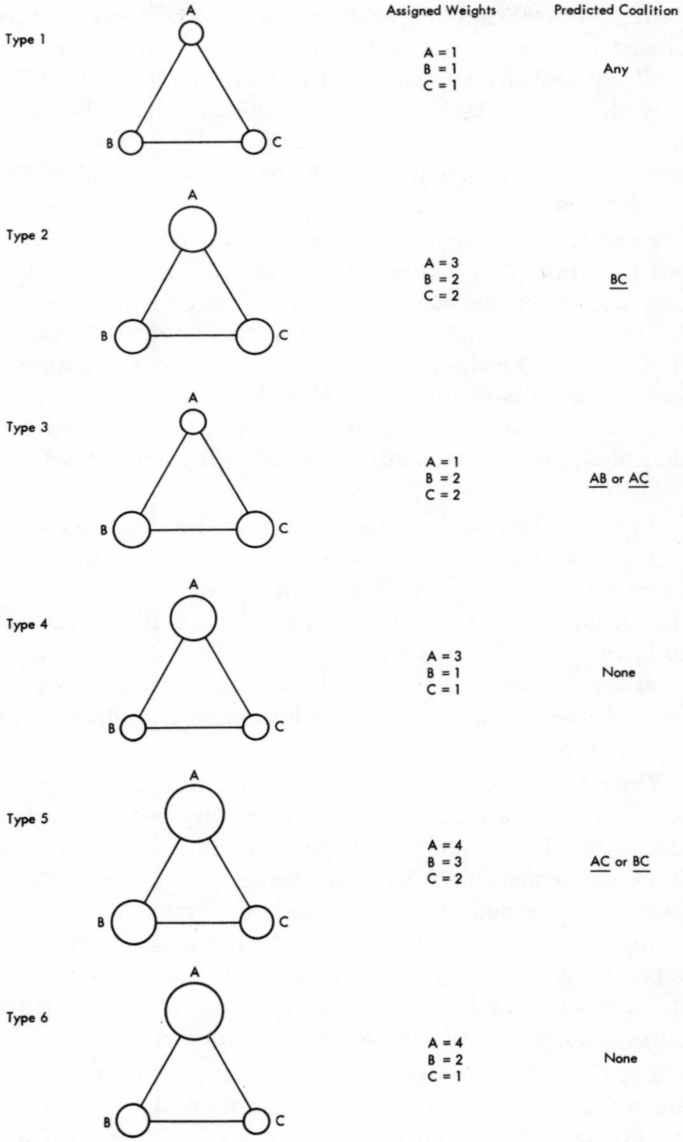

		Assigned Weights	Predicted Coalition
Type 1		A = 1 B = 1 C = 1	Any
Type 2		A = 3 B = 2 C = 2	<u>BC</u>
Type 3		A = 1 B = 2 C = 2	<u>AB</u> or <u>AC</u>
Type 4		A = 3 B = 1 C = 1	None
Type 5		A = 4 B = 3 C = 2	<u>AC</u> or <u>BC</u>
Type 6		A = 4 B = 2 C = 1	None

[4] After Vinacke and Arkoff, *op. cit.*

is unequivocally disadvantageous. However, the three possible coalitions are no longer of equal advantage. Consider the position of *B*. If he forms a coalition with *A*, he will (by virtue of the coalition) be stronger than *C*, but within the coalition he will be weaker than *A*. If, on the other hand, he forms a coalition with *C*, he will be equal to *C* within the coalition and stronger than *A* by virtue of the coalition. The position of *C* is identical with that of *B*, so that other things being equal, the coalition *BC* will be formed and the individually strongest member of the triad will ordinarily turn out to be the weakest after the formation of the most probable coalition.

Type 3. Here again, two members of the triad are equal in strength, but this time the third member is weaker. It will readily be seen that *A* may strengthen his position by forming a coalition with either *B* or *C*, and will be welcomed as an ally by either *B* or *C*. On the other hand, if *B* joins *C*, he does not improve his precoalition position of equality with *C* and superiority to *A*. His only motive to enter a coalition with *C* is to block the coalition *AC*. However, *C*'s position is identical with that of *B*, and he, too, will prefer *A* to *B* as an ally. Thus there are two probable coalitions, *AB* and *AC*.

Type 4. In this case, the strength of *A* exceeds the combined strength of *B* and *C*. *B* and *C* have no motive to form a coalition with each other. Once formed, such a coalition would still be weaker than *A* alone, and they would still be equal within it. On the other hand *A* has no motive to form a coalition with *B* or *C*, since he is already stronger than either of them and is not threatened by their coalition. No coalition will be formed unless either *B* or *C* can find some extraneous means of inducing *A* to join him.

Type 5. In· this case, no two members of the triad are equal in strength but the combined strength of any two members exceeds that of the third. This resembles Type 3 in that the weakest member of the triad has a definite advantage, being sure to be included in whatever coalition is formed. *A* seeks to join both *B* and *C*, and *C* seeks to join both *A* and *B*, but *B* has no incentive to enter a coalition with *A* and *A* has a very strong incentive to enter a coalition with *C*. Whether the differential strength of *A* and *B* will make them differentially attractive to *C* lies outside the scope of our present assumptions.

Type 6. This is like Type 5 in that the three members of the triad are unequal, but here *A* is stronger than *B* and *C* combined and has no motive to form a coalition. As in Type 4, true coalition is impossible.

Table 3–1 shows the results obtained by Vinacke and Arkoff when their student subjects played ninety games of each type. In general, the results conformed to the theoretical expectations. In Type 1, all three coalitions

TABLE 3–1

Coalitions Formed in the Six Types of Power Patterns in Triads [5]

Allies	Type 1 (1-1-1)	Type 2 (3-2-2)	Type 3 (1-2-2)	Type 4 (3-1-1)	Type 5 (4-3-2)	Type 6 (4-2-1)
AB	33	13	24	11	9	9
AC	17	12	40	10	20	13
BC	30	64	15	7	59	8
Total	80	89	79	28	88	30
(No Coalition)	10	1	11	62	2	60
P	>.05	<.10	<.01	<.70	<.01	<.50

[5] Vinacke and Arkoff, *op. cit.*, p. 409.

occurred frequently, although the experimenters could not explain why *AC* is under-represented and neither can we.

In Type 2 the predicted coalition *BC* is by far the most frequent. In Type 3 the predicted coalitions *AB* and *AC* are most frequent, although there is an unexplained difference between them. In Types 4 and 6 no coalitions are anticipated by the theory, and in most of the games played no coalitions occurred.

Either an *AC* or *BC* coalition was anticipated for Type 5, and these were the most frequent outcomes. The *BC* coalition was significantly more frequent than the *AC*. This was not entirely unexpected. The theory anticipated the possibility that *C,* the weaker partner in either of the probable coalitions, might prefer a lesser margin of inferiority and therefore choose *B* over *A*.

The possibility that these patterns were based on participants' unfamiliarity with the game and would disappear with practice could be tested by comparing the results in successive games played by the same subjects. There were no significant shifts in outcome from first game to last, but it was observed that players did learn about the necessity of forming coalitions in Types 1, 2, 3, and 5, and the futility of forming them in Types 4 and 6. Most of the noncoalitions in the former types occurred in the first series of games, as did more of the coalitions in the latter types.

The experimenters noted which player initiated the offer to form each winning coalition and how the prize was divided. The prize, a hundred points per game, was divided by agreement between the winning partners. Not unexpectedly, the weaker players were quickest to propose coalitions. The published data on the division of rewards is incomplete, but

. . . the conclusion is warranted that players made deals in accordance with perceived strength, with the result that those having the same weight divided the prize equally, and those having different weights made disproportionate agreements.[6]

The experimenters were mildly troubled by these results, which they considered to be irrational since if any two players can form a winning coalition, no player is a better or worse coalition partner than another, and the assigned weights are really irrelevant. They were gently tolerant of their subjects' apparent delusion:

> It must be remembered that people tend to act according to their perceptions of a situation, and not according to what a fully informed theorist might expect. People play games, very often, according to the apparently advantageous strategy rather than the strategy they ought to follow. In our game situation, they played the way they thought they had to play in order to win. It happens, apparently, that they played in terms of the initial distribution of strength, rather than in terms of purely rational analysis of outcome.[7]

The impression that the behavior observed in these experimental triads is irrational can be dispelled by an afternoon's play of this form of pachisi. It will be found that although any player is indispensable when he participates in a winning coalition, the coalitions are not equally indispensable to the players. Thus, if no coalition is formed in the Type 5 triad, *A* wins. He has less incentive than his fellows to form a coalition, and it is not irrational for him to make and accept fewer offers than the others. The other feature of the game that emerges in actual play is that the "rational" strategy whereby each player considers the other two as equally unattractive partners and invites them to bid against each other for his support leads to infinitely prolonged bidding with no equilibrium point. For example, if *A* and *B* have tentatively agreed on a coalition with a 50/50 division of the reward, *C* may propose an *AC* coalition with a 60/40 division in *A*'s favor. *B* may counter with an offer of a 50/50 *BC* coalition which *A* may outbid in turn by offering 60/40 to either of the others. If the players demonstrate the "strict rationality" demanded of them the bidding never ceases; no coalition is ever formed and no game is played to the end.[8] The players could evade this pitfall by adopting the convention that any offer of an even division is acceptable, but under that rule each player would be confronted with two identical offers and would have no rational basis of choice between them. Like the ass of Buridan, he must find an irra-

---

[6] *Ibid.,* p. 412.

[7] *Ibid.,* p. 413.

[8] An experiment in which such a situation actually occurred is reported by Bernhardt Lieberman in "i-Trust: A Notion of Trust in Three-Person Games and International Affairs," *Journal of Conflict Resolution,* V (1964), 271–80.

tional principle of selection or remain immobile between two equal opportunities. It is not so easy to devise a tactically sound form of irrationality. A player who decides to choose his coalition partner at random, perhaps by tossing a coin, is defenseless against random exclusion by the other pair, or even worse, their development of a nonrandom preference for each other.

Another alternative is to choose one's coalition partner for some reason that is unrelated to the game. But this is a pointless tactic unless the preference is reciprocated, which is not likely unless the third player is neutralized or the chosen partner is offered inducements outside the framework of the game. Although both these conditions occur in real life, they do not conform to the rules of the experiment. The subjects' use of the assigned weights to regulate the bidding process resolves these paradoxes and enables the game to proceed.

THE STRYKER-PSATHAS GAME

Stryker and Psathas [9] experimented with a pachisi game involving only triads of Type 3. Twelve groups of student subjects played twelve games each and the power distribution was again based on assigned weights. Type 3 triads have two strong players and a weak player; the weight of the weak player was varied to see how this would affect the subjects' divisions of the prize.

The Stryker-Psathas game has several special rules that transform its character and give us a clearer view of the motives underlying "irrational" coalition strategies. The first is that ties are not permitted. Players who tie are forced to replay the game until the tie is broken. In Type 3 triads this makes coalitions compulsory. If no coalition is formed, the two strong players tie and are sent back to play the game properly. This rule eliminates the alternative strategy open to strong players of avoiding coalitions and playing the game alone to the end. Any player, whether weak or strong, must join a coalition in order to obtain a share of the prize. All possible coalitions should occur with equal frequency, and the tendency for weak players to be preferred as coalition partners should disappear. This is what occurred in the experimental games played without constraints: the weak man was included in coalitions with a frequency exactly equal to chance.

The other special rule is somewhat more complicated. The free formation of coalitions was permitted in only one of the four series of games played, with the remaining games being governed by arbitrary constraints,

[9] Sheldon Stryker and George Psathas, "Research on Coalitions in the Triad: Findings, Problems, and Strategy," *Sociometry*, XXIII, No. 3 (September 1960), pp. 217–30.

FIGURE 3-2

The Stryker-Psathas Game[10]

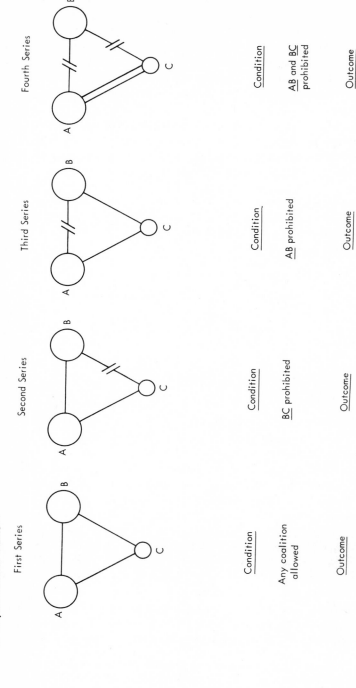

First Series

Condition

Any coalition allowed

Outcome

Equal frequency of AB, BC, and AC coalitions

Second Series

Condition

BC prohibited

Outcome

AC coalition two out of three times

Third Series

Condition

AB prohibited

Outcome

AC and BC coalitions

Fourth Series

Condition

AB and BC prohibited

Outcome

AC coalition in every game

[10] After Stryker and Psathas, *ibid.*

28

as shown in Figure 3–2. In the first series all three coalitions were allowed. In the second series player *A* [11] enjoyed an absolute choice between partners *B* and *C*, inasmuch as the formation of a coalition was forced and the *BC* coalition was prohibited. In the third series *C* was the chooser, the *AB* coalition being prohibited. In the fourth series the *AC* coalition was compulsory. The published report furnishes information on the proportion of the prize received by *C* in each series and with each of three different assigned weights.

There are indications that the subjects did not completely understand the instructions, or that they resisted them:

> In some games played by some triads, players tossed the die to determine who would coalesce with whom; some even went so far as to toss the die to determine the division of the prize among the partners.[12]

The results are nevertheless interesting. In the first series the two strong players chose the weak player twice as often as they chose each other, but only on the basis of the weak player's willingness to accept a lesser share of the prize. In the second series, in which *A* alone was the chooser, *C* was again chosen two out of three times on the same terms. *C*'s average share was 34 per cent in the first series and 35 per cent in the second series.

In the third series of trials *C* was in the strongest position, enjoying an uncontrolled choice of coalition partners. His average share of the prize was 53 per cent, but this average conceals differences among several types of players:

> *Extortionate.* In eight games *C* demanded and got 85 per cent or more of the prize.
> *Exploitative.* In four games *C* took between 60 and 75 per cent of the prize.
> *Generous.* Ten *C*'s divided the prize evenly with their helpless opponents.
> *Confused.* Fourteen *C*'s negotiated an arrangement whereby they received less than an even share.

In the fourth series, when the coalition *AC* was, in effect, made compulsory, most of the *C*'s negotiated an approximately even division with *A*, but a substantial minority took less than half for themselves. We do not know what constraint compelled *A* and *C* to reach an agreement on the division of the prize in this fourth series, but it obviously must have worked to the disadvantage of *C*. In replicating this experiment in a Columbia University seminar, we discovered that negotiations sometimes

---

[11] Stryker and Psathas used the letters *s* (for *strong*) and *w* (for *weak*) to label their players. For easier comprehension we have returned to the usual labels of *A*, *B*, and *C*.
[12] Stryker and Psathas, *op. cit.*, p. 229.

broke down entirely when *C* insisted on an equal share—because the game could not be continued without the formation of an *AC* coalition and some *A*'s were adamant in their insistence on receiving a larger share.

THE KELLEY-ARROWOOD GAME

This question of rationality in coalition formation was further explored in two experiments by Kelley and Arrowood.[13] Ninety subjects were asked to play the Vinacke-Arkoff game under conditions intended to reduce misunderstanding and to maximize their comprehension of the basic strategical issues. Only the Type 5 triad was used, and only a single set of weights (4–3–2). Each subject played the game many times and the instructions were comprehensive and detailed. These procedures were expected to reduce the "illusion" of *A*'s greater power and the tendency for *BC* coalitions to form in this type of triad. The experimenters also anticipated that players would become more "rational" over a long series of trials, moving towards equal divisions of the prize. These expectations were partly fulfilled. The predominance of the *BC* coalitions was less than in previous experiments with Type 5 triads and it declined slightly as the subjects became more experienced. The tendency of coalition partners to partition prizes in proportion to their own assigned weights also diminished to some extent.

At the conclusion of the experiment the subjects filled out a questionnaire about their subjective reactions. From these responses the experimenters concluded that the attribution of power to the player with the highest assigned weight might reflect either a realistic pessimism of the other players about the possibility of organizing a coalition against him or the belief that an actor's effectiveness when acting for himself is an appropriate measure of his potential contribution to a cooperative effort.

For their second experiment Kelley and Arrowood designed a game in which "real" power differences between the players were created by giving each player an alternative reward if he failed to gain membership in a coalition, or if once in a coalition, he was unable to agree with his partner on the division of the reward. In this condition the player with the higher weight would have less need to enter into a coalition, but once a coalition was formed, he could bargain more effectively because he would have less to lose than if no agreement could be reached. As anticipated, the preference for *BC* coalitions in the Type 5 triad was greater in the second experiment than in the first, and this preference seemed to increase with experience.

[13] Harold H. Kelley and A. John Arrowood, "Coalitions in the Triad: Critique and Experiment," *Sociometry*, XXIII, No. 3 (September 1960), 231–44.

VINACKE'S LATER EXPERIMENTS

Meanwhile, Vinacke and his students had embarked on a series of experiments to determine the effect of player characteristics on patterns of coalition formation. Their first experiment [14] compared two sets of all-male triads and two sets of all-female triads, composed as before of student subjects. One set of each sex played the standard Vinacke-Arkoff game with its three repetitions of six power patterns. The other set played the same game but with the addition of a record sheet showing the total number of points earned by each player as the session progressed. This cumulative score was kept in view at all times.

The introduction of a cumulative score, as Vinacke reported elsewhere,[15] makes the assigned weights irrelevant. The cumulative scores posted at the beginning of each round of play become the effective weights instead. As soon as any player develops a substantial lead, a coalition between the two losing players becomes almost inevitable. The joint interest of the losers has self-evident priority over any competition between themselves until they come within striking distance of the leading player. Very little information can be gleaned from the reported behavior of triads playing with cumulative scores unless we know how the scores stand at each moment of the experiment.

This particular study illustrates a familiar problem in social psychology. The experimenter, who had the advantage of observing his subjects directly and reading the notes of other observers, emerged with the conviction that male and female players have distinctly different styles of play, women being

> . . . less concerned with arriving at a fair and friendly solution to the problem. The task for them appears to be to determine a way in which no one suffers at the expense of anyone else.[16]

This conclusion is heavily dependent upon statistical differences that are not significant. In the course of analysis the meaning of statistical significance is eventually forgotten, and differences in the expected direction are accepted as evidence even though they fail the experimenter's own test for admissibility. Thus we read:

> Little difference occurs for Types 3–1–1 and 4–2–1, but there is a large, although not significant, difference for the combined results in patterns where

14 W. Edgar Vinacke, "Sex Roles in a Three-Person Game," *Sociometry*, XXII, No. 4 (December 1959), 343–60.

15 W. Edgar Vinacke, "The Effects of Cumulative Score on Coalition Formation in Triads with Various Patterns of Internal Power," *American Psychologist*, XIV (July 1959), p. 381.

16 Vinacke, "Sex Roles in a Three-Person Game," *op. cit.*, p. 357.

only two can win . . . since males engage more frequently in extended bargaining sequences.[17]

And elsewhere:

Although significant at the 5-per-cent level in only one comparison, there is a consistent tendency for females to offer to form an alliance more frequently in Types 3–1–1 and 4–2–1, when none is necessary. In Type 4–3–2 the reverse takes place, with the weakest member less likely to make an offer among female members. Again, the same picture emerges under Cumulative Score Conditions, but so much reduced as not to attain statistical significance.[18]

Lacking the impressions gained from direct observation I cannot discern in Vinacke's meticulous tables the difference in strategic style between the sexes that he claims to have found. In his own words,

. . . it is evident from Table 1 that both sexes strikingly follow the general strategy previously reported for male groups, namely, the two weakest members tend to ally against the stronger, when this is possible.[19]

There were *no* significant differences when cumulative scores were shown. The only significant differences that appear in the game-by-game condition were that women players formed more triple alliances in some types of triads, and formed somewhat fewer coalitions throughout the series of games. On the other hand, unequal divisions of the prize were significantly more frequent in male coalitions. Men took greater advantage of their assigned weights when arranging to divide a prize.

These findings are interesting even if they do not quite support the experimenters' preconceived notion of pliant, accommodating females and brutally competitive males. The female players seem to have understood the game less and to have taken its rules and conditions less seriously. Whether this actually reflects less interest in competitive games or less sensitivity to status ranking is difficult to say, but both suppositions are reasonable, and the differences are slight in any case.

Another interesting attempt to relate player characteristics to coalition formation was reported from the same laboratory in 1960.[20] Twenty triads of male students were recruited from classes that had already been given psychological tests of Achievement ("the desire to overcome obstacles, exercise power, and to strive to do something difficult as well and as quickly as possible"[21]) and Nurturance ("the need to nourish, aid or

[17] *Ibid.,* p. 356.

[18] *Ibid.,* p. 351.

[19] *Ibid.,* pp. 348–49.

[20] Marilyn V. Chaney and W. Edgar Vinacke, "Achievement and Nurturance in Triads Varying in Power Distribution," *Journal of Abnormal and Social Psychology,* LX, No. 2 (March 1960), 176–81.

[21] *Ibid.,* p. 176.

protect the helpless, to express sympathy" [22]). The sample was arranged so that each triad included one subject high in achievement and low in nurturance, another subject high in nurturance and low in achievement, and a third, or control, subject with intermediate scores for both characteristics.

The results were inconclusive. Success or failure in the competition seemed to depend much more on luck in drawing weights than on the personalities of the players. Subjects with high achievement scores were somewhat more active in precoalition bargaining and may have used their opportunities somewhat more fully than the subjects with high nurturance scores (although less effectively than the control subjects). However, the observed differences were trivial. Either the personality tests were defective or the characteristics that they measure have little influence on a player's style.

Vinacke and his collaborators continued [23] the attempt to delineate typically masculine and feminine strategies and eventually devised an "index of feminine strategy" based upon six propensities supposedly displayed by women in Vinacke-Arkoff pachisi: (1) to form triple coalitions, (2) to refuse to form coalitions, (3) to divide prizes equally instead of proportionately, (4) to form coalitions in situations in which no coalition is necessary to win, (5) to refuse to bargain, and (6) to suggest strategies for their opponents. The tables in the first of these papers are exceedingly hard to read and the numerical results are given in a form that does not permit the reader to make independent calculations. Some differences between the sexes are apparent in the results; but they are not very large nor entirely consistent. Recognizing that such differences might merely show female sophomores to be less interested in pachisi than male sophomores, Uesugi and Vinacke proposed a triadic game emphasizing feminine interests. Weights were drawn in the usual fashion, and the same series of triadic types was used, but points were obtained by answering the successive questions of a quiz rather than by a throw of dice. The quiz was feminine in both content and style. A sample question follows:

Question: "When a girl is asked to dinner by a train acquaintance, she should—
     1. Call the conductor.
     2. Dash for the dining room.
     3. Go Dutch.

Correct Answer: No harm in casual chatter to while the miles away—when the Handsome Stranger's not the wolf type. A girl who accepts

22 *Ibid.*
23 John R. Bond and W. Edgar Vinacke, "Coalitions in Mixed Sex Triads," *Sociometry*, XXIV, No. 1 (March 1961), 61–75; and Thomas K. Uesugi and W. Edgar Vinacke, "Strategy in a Feminine Game," *Sociometry*, XXV, No. 1 (March 1962), 75–88.

his dining car bid should GO DUTCH—then she needn't feel indebted." [24]

The experimenters sum up the findings of this attempt to validate the "distinctive features of feminine accommodative strategy" as follows:

Triple Alliances.   Just as in the "masculine game," so in the "feminine" quiz game, the female triads agree more often to form triple alliances (by X^2, this difference falls short of significance in both cases, P .05). . . .

Failure to Form Coalitions.   In the "feminine" game, there was a slight and non-significant decline on this index for both sexes. . . .

Equal Division of the Prize.   The results for this measure are similar to triple alliances, except that only a very slight difference between the two games was found for male triads. In contrast, the female triads show a very considerable increase in this outcome in the feminine game ($X^2 = 7.85$, $P<.01$). . . .

Coalitions in the All-Powerful Pattern.   No significant differences between the two games occurred, insofar as formation of coalitions is concerned. . . .

Amount of Bargaining.   No significant differences were found.

The sixth measure, number of altruistic offers, was not analyzed separately, since the total incidence of such offers was too small to permit statistical analysis.[25]

Cheerfully determined not to let the wings of theory be clipped by the scissors of empirical data, the investigators arrived at the astonishing conclusion that:

The results of this experiment point to the decided probability that strategy varies with the relevance of the situation to the characteristics of the players. It is quite striking to find that accommodative strategy apparently becomes more sharply defined in a game intended to enhance feminine interests.[26]

WILLIS' TETRADIC GAME

Another variant of pachisi was developed by Willis,[27] who attempted to extend the theory of coalition formation to tetrads by playing four-handed pachisi. His subjects were 144 Finnish students divided into all-male and all-female tetrads. The pachisi board had 100 squares. The player or coalition first reaching the end of the board received 100 points, and each player was to accumulate as many points as possible in a series of twenty games.

Willis' pachisi differs from the Vinache-Arkoff game in one very significant way. In the latter, all players move on the same throw of the die, causing the player with the highest assigned weight inevitably to win

---

24 Uesugi and Vinacke, *ibid.,* p. 82.

25 *Ibid.,* pp. 84–85.

26 *Ibid.,* pp. 85–86.

27 Richard H. Willis, "Coalitions in the Tetrad," *Sociometry,* XXV, No. 4 (December 1962), 358–76.

in individual play. In the same way, when a coalition is formed the outcome of the game is immediately predetermined; chance plays no part. Willis' game is closer to conventional pachisi. Each player moves in turn and on his own throw. This reintroduces the element of chance, which is augmented still more by the rule that moves can only be made on an even number. When an odd number is thrown, the player loses his move on that turn. According to these rules every game must be played to the end, since any player or coalition has some hope of winning.

Willis identifies seventeen types of tetrad and predicts the most likely two-way and three-way coalitions in each type. Table 3–1 is taken from his paper. The reader may determine for himself that power distributions are much more difficult to visualize in tetrads than in triads.[28]

A surprising feature of Willis' table is his inclusion of coalitions with superfluous members. The original theory and all of the experiments with triads assumed that coalitions would ordinarily be formed to command a majority of the assigned weight, i.e., a winning share of the total available power. Although the concept of the *minimum winning coalition* had not yet been formulated, it was expected that triads would usually develop coalitions of two against one rather than triple alliances.

Most of the predicted three-way coalitions in Table 3–1 include a superfluous member. Thus in Type 3, all the predicted three-way coalitions, *ABC, ACD,* and *BCD,* would command a majority of power without the superfluous partner *D.* Similarly, in Type 7 the predicted three-way coalitions *ACD* and *BCD* do not require *D* for a majority. In Type 9 one predicted three-way coalition *ABD* includes a superfluous member and the other, *ACD,* offers a choice of superfluous members—either *C* or *D* can be spared.

Willis' Helsinki experiment was run on tetrads of Types 7 and 9. Each player held the same weight in the same type of tetrad throughout the experiment. Half the subjects were assigned to a Type 7 situation (4–4–3–2) and the other half to a Type 9 situation (5–3–3–2).

The results were inconclusive with respect to the predicted coalitions, as might be expected from the large element of chance in the game. Players seem to have estimated correctly that any coalition might win but that coalitions with slight majorities of power would be more economical than overwhelming coalitions. Excluding minority coalitions and countercoalitions, the predicted two-way coalitions accounted for 54 per cent of all coalitions actually formed in Type 7 triads, and 70 per cent of those formed in Type 9 triads.

---

28 Karlsson has proposed a mathematical formula for winning coalitions that would reduce this complexity, but at the cost of introducing additional assumptions. See George Karlsson, "Some Aspects of Power in Small Groups," in Joan H. Criswell, *et al.,* eds., *Mathematical Methods in Small Group Processes* (Stanford, Calif.: Stanford University Press, 1962), pp. 193–202.

TABLE 3–1

Predictions Yielded by Extended Caplovian Theory [29]

Power Relations				No	Predicted Coalitions Two-Way	Predicted Coalitions Three-Way
A>B + C + D				1	None	None
A ≤ B + C + D	A = B = C = D			2	All equally frequent	All equally frequent
	A = B = C>D			3	AB, AC, BC	ABD, ACD, BCD
	A>B = C = D	A = B + C + D		4	AB, AC, AD	All equally frequent*
		A<B + C + D		5		BCD
	A = B>C = D			6	AB	ACD, BCD
	A = B>C>D			7	AC, BC	
	A > B = C > D	A = B + C + D		8	AB, AC, AD	ABC, ACD
		A < B + C + D	A + D>B + C	9		BCD
			A + D = B + C	10	AB, AC	
			A + D<B + C	11	BC	
	A >B >C = D	A = B + C + D		12	AB, AC, AD	ACD
		A<B + C + D		13		ACD, BCD
	A > B > C>D	A = B + C + D		14	AB, AC, AD	No prediction†
		A < B + C + D	A + D>B + C	15		ACD, BCD
			A + D = B + C	16	AB, AC	
			A + D<B + C	17	AC, BC	

* Perhaps BCD less frequent, although it meets the formal requirement.
† No three-way coalition meets the formal requirement.

GAMSON'S THEORY

The theory of coalition formation was considerably refined by Gamson in a paper published in 1961.[30] His first contribution was an improvement in the terminology of coalition formation:

[29] Reproduced unchanged from Table 1 in Willis' "Coalitions in the Tetrad," *op. cit.*, p. 361.

[30] William A. Gamson, "A Theory of Coalition Formation," *American Sociological Review*, XXVI, No. 3 (June 1961), 373–82. The quotation that follows is from p. 374. See also his closely related paper, "An Experimental Test of a Theory of Coalition Formation," *American Sociological Review*, XXVI, No. 4 (August 1961), 565–73.

A *decision* is a selection among alternatives. . . . A *social unit* is any individual or group which for the duration of the decision follows the same
coalition strategy. It might be a state delegation to a political convention, a
voting bloc in the United Nations, or an association of retail stores. A *coalition* is the joint use of resources by two or more social units. Once formed, a
coalition will frequently meet the definition of a social unit from the period
of formation until the decision has been made. A *winning* coalition is one
with sufficient resources to control the decision. The *decision point* is the
minimum proportion of resources necessary to control the decision.

He also introduced the useful concepts of the *minimal winning coalition,* the *cheapest winning coalition,* and *nonutilitarian strategy preferences.* A minimal winning coalition is "a winning coalition such that
the defection of any member will make the coalition no longer winning."
The cheapest winning coalition is "that minimal winning coalition with
total resources closest to the decision point." [31] This distinction is worth
remembering, since the term minimal winning coalition has been widely
used in recent discussion to describe the cheapest coalition. All two-way
coalitions are minimal in all games where the outcome is affected by the
formation of a coalition. In a tetrad, as we have seen, it is possible to
identify nonminimal winning three-way coalitions that include one or
more minimal two-way coalitions.

The nonutilitarian strategy preferences of players are their inclinations
to form coalitions with other players for reasons unrelated to the other
players' control of resources. The sources of such preferences, of course,
vary according to the situation and according to the character of the
social unit involved: ". . . in a small committee," Gamson remarks, "the
primary source would probably be interpersonal attraction. In a political
convention, we would expect the relative similarity of others' ideology
and beliefs to be the principal determinant." [32]

The hub of Gamson's theory is a psychological assumption and a
strategical corollary. The assumption reads as follows:

Any participant will expect others to demand from a coalition a share of the
payoff proportional to the amount of resources which they contribute to a
coalition.[33]

Gamson describes this as an empirical hypothesis. On the whole it is
well supported by the various pachisi experiments and seems plausible.
Whether a more solid basis for it can be found remains to be seen. We
might call this assumption the Equitable Expectation. Its strategical consequences are elegantly deduced by Gamson:

31 Gamson, "A Theory of Coalition Formation," *ibid.,* p. 376.
32 *Ibid.,* p. 375.
33 *Ibid.,* p. 376.

When a player must choose among alternative coalition strategies where the total payoff to a winning coalition is constant, he will maximize his payoff by maximizing his share. The theory states that he will do this by maximizing the ratio of his resources to the total resources of the coalition. Since his resources will be the same regardless of which coalition he joins, the lower the total resources, the greater will be his share. Thus, where the total payoff is held constant, he will favor the cheapest winning coalition.* [34]

He continues by showing that the application of this principle to the continuous situation in the eight basic types of triads changes one of my predictions. For the Type 5 triad, always of particular interest, the principle of the cheapest winning coalition predicts a *BC* coalition rather than "either *BC* or *AC*."

Using the data of the original Vinacke and Arkoff study, Gamson is able to show that *BC* coalitions actually occurred more frequently than *AC* coalitions in Type 5 games. This finding has been replicated several times.

William Riker has worked out a much fuller statement about the advantages of the cheapest winning coalition, based both on mathematical inference and on empirical data from American political history. He calls it the Size Principle and states it thus:

> In social situations similar to *n*-person, zero-sum games with side-payments, participants create coalitions just as large as they believe will ensure winning and no larger.[35]

A table of predicted coalitions for given power distributions in triads and tetrads is included in the same work.

THE EQUITABLE EXPECTATION

How reliable is the Equitable Expectation? We have reviewed the struggles of various scholars with the apparent contradiction between rational solutions of triadic games and solutions based on players' assigned weights. The Equitable Expectation may be construed to be a statement about human nature, or at least about human nature in Western societies. It seems to involve the players' lifetime experiments in decision-making as well as their tactics in a particular game. Kelley and Arrowood asked their subjects after the experiment why they feared or respected the

---

* But one recent experiment shows results that are not entirely consistent with the hypothesis. See William R. Morgan and Jack Sawyer, "Bargaining, Expectations, and the Preference for Equality Over Equity," *Journal of Personality and Social Psychology*, VI, No. 2, 1967, pp. 139–49.

[34] Gamson, *op. cit.*, p. 376.

[35] William H. Riker, *The Theory of Political Coalitions* (New Haven: Yale University Press, 1962), p. 47.

TABLE 3–2

Predicted Coalitions in Various Types of Triads

Type	Cheapest Winning Coalitions (Gamson)[36]	Available Revolutionary Coalitions
1	Any	Any
2	BC	BC
3	AB or AC	AB or AC
4	None	None
5	BC	BC
6	None	None
7	Inapplicable[37]	None
8	Inapplicable	None

player with the highest assigned weight. That player's certainty of winning the game if no coalitions were formed was the reason most often mentioned, but many responses seemed to refer to ". . . previous experience in games that higher numbers are generally better ones and in everyday life that quantity often has the upper hand." [38] Another group of players amplified deference into systematic error; they convinced themselves that the rules of the game compelled them to accept offers from the leading player. And a few subjects suggested that players with higher weights were entitled to larger shares of the reward because they contributed more to the game.

Most, if not all, status systems seem to embody the double principle of unequal rewards and unequal contributions so that some counterpart of the Equitable Expectation is found in most organizations, based on one or another of the following themes:

If the cooperative effort were dissolved and replaced by competition or conflict, the actor with the greatest resources would be able to increase his share of all prizes and might even be able to exclude the other actors entirely. He therefore deserves gratitude for his forbearance in addition to his disproportionate share of available rewards.

An actor's effectiveness when acting alone is an index to his relative effectiveness in joint action. Common experience suggests that the weight a man can lift or haul alone is a good measure of his usefulness in a group of men lifting or hauling together.

Groups of men lifting or hauling are likely to undertake tasks that are

---

36 Adapted from Gamson, "A Theory of Coalition Formation," *op. cit.*, p. 377.

37 Types 7 and 8 are labeled "inapplicable" by Gamson because they do not meet one of his technical conditions, i.e., that no participant must be indispensable to every winning coalition.

38 Kelley and Arrowood, *op. cit.*, p. 236.

nearly beyond their collective capacity, so that the marginal contribution of one strong man will often determine success or failure. That man, like Achilles, may claim credit for the total achievement.

As we have seen in the pachisi experiments, the need to choose among alternative partners and to agree on the division of prizes often leads players to formulate rules about the choice of partners and the division of prizes from whatever materials come readiest to hand. The relative distribution of resources is always a convenient framework for the assignment of new tasks and the division of new prizes. Thus a status order, once established, tends to reinforce itself by reproducing previous inequalities in new transactions between the individual and the collectivity.

These considerations do not enable us to prove the Equitable Expectation rigorously, but they do suggest that whatever we succeed in learning about the basic properties of triadic games [39] may be useful in understanding much larger and more intricate social systems.

[39] In addition to the pachisi studies, a number of experimenters have devised triadic games requiring the cooperative performance of tasks. See, among others, Paul H. Hoffman, *et al.*, "Tendencies Toward Group Comparability in Competitive Bargaining," *Human Relations*, VII (1954), 141–59; Leonard Berkowitz, *et al.*, "Effects of Performance Evaluations on Group Integration and Motivation," *Human Relations*, X (1957), 194–208; Theodore M. Mills, *et al.*, *Group Structure and the Newcomer: An Experimental Study of Group Expansion* (Oslo: Oslo University Press, 1957); Loren J. Chapman and Donald T. Campbell, "An Attempt to Predict the Performance of Three-Man Teams from Attitude Measures," *Journal of Social Psychology*, XLVI (1957), 277–86; and Jean-Pierre Poitou, "Perception des contributions individuelles au travail de groupe dans une structure social hiérarchisée," *Psychologie Française*, IX, No. 4 (1964), 304–15.

IV

APISH TRICKS

Primates, including man, differ from other mammals in that they have hands and feet that can grasp objects firmly. Other animals have claws or hooves and cannot easily modify their environments. A monkey is vastly superior to the most intelligent dog in coping with change. The dog cannot even brush the hair away from his eyes when his vision is obscured. The monkey can lift, pry, poke, squeeze, push, and pull. He can take things apart, and put them together again. Monkeys use tools, and fulfill obligations to their relatives.

The modern student of primate behavior goes to the natural habitat of monkeys or apes armed with pencil, notebook, and wristwatch, sometimes with binoculars and camera, to observe the behavior of the apes under normal conditions. Few academic fields call for so much patience and courage. There are nearly 200 species of living primates, and according to DeVore:

> . . . there are reliable field studies of the behavior of less than one dozen. Of the usually recognized families of primates, that of the apes, the Pongidae (gibbon, orangutan, chimpanzee, and gorilla) is the only one in which a majority of the genera have been the subject of systematic, continued observation under natural conditions.[1]

1 Irven DeVore, ed., *Primate Behavior* (New York: Holt, Rinehart & Winston, Inc., 1965), p. 6.

Yet much is already known about primate behavior that could never have been discovered by studying captive animals in the zoo or in the laboratory.[2] All of the apes and most of the monkeys are social animals, living their entire lives in close association with what would be described in human company as relatives, friends, or neighbors. The size and structure of primate groups vary with the species and also appear to vary with the locale.[3]

These groups are genuinely social. Membership is fairly stable, less persistent perhaps than in a human family, but comparable to a street corner gang or a suburban neighborhood. They have well-defined hierarchies based primarily on age and sex and secondarily on individual characteristics. For example, among the mountain gorillas observed by Schaller,[4] silver-backed males always dominate adult females, and adult females always dominate juveniles, allowing for some contention between black-backed (young adult) males and adult females. Among silver-backed males in the same group, there is a fixed status order. Adult females seem to have variable status; mothers with young infants are favored. Among juvenile gorillas, dominance is based on size and strength.

Within all of the primate groups observed so far, there are well-defined family roles, and a pattern of collective activity that protects weaker members from predators. There is substantial evidence of group learning—a kind of rudimentary culture. When baboons are attacked by men or alligators, the entire group, including individuals absent at the time of the attack, learn to avoid the place or circumstances associated with the danger, and do so for a long period of time.

Primate groups are strikingly cohesive. Their members are involved in a dense network of relationships that strongly resembles a human primary group. Each animal seems to recognize every other member of his group as an individual and small groups can attend large camp meetings without merging or losing their identities. The observation of rhesus monkeys living on the grounds of one Indian temple disclosed four separate groups that intermingled only rarely and briefly, although they occupied the same territory.

There appears to be enormous variation in sexual activity among the primates, from the gorillas, who copulate rarely and without visible

[2] For an experimental comparison of the two sorts of data, see William A. Mason, "The Effects of Environmental Restriction on the Social Development of Rhesus Monkeys," in *Primate Social Behavior,* ed. Charles H. Southwick (Princeton, New Jersey: D. Van Nostrand Company, Inc., 1963), pp. 161–73.

[3] Baboons, for example, seem to form one type of community in Ethiopia and another type entirely in Kenya.

[4] George B. Schaller, "The Behavior of the Mountain Gorillas," Chap. 10 in DeVore, ed., *op. cit.* See esp. Table 10-3, p. 346.

enthusiasm, to the baboons, who do little else.[5] But in every species studied, access to females is regulated by the hierarchy established among adult males. Female primates and their young usually live in a group controlled by one or more adult males, who mate with the females and protect the young according to the manner of their species, but generally in such a way that the more dominant males do more mating and more protecting. Some males, particularly younger animals, live in celibate isolation or on the periphery of a group.

Peace is the normal condition within most primate groups, with easy egress for the dissatisfied. Further observation may correct these impressions, but to date it appears that we are less peaceable in intimate relationships than our anthropoid cousins, perhaps because we have so much more property and pride at stake.

There appears to be no single norm for intergroup conflict. For example, the howler monkeys show consistent hostility to strangers of their own species, gorillas are suspicious but not aggressive towards outsiders, and chimpanzees mingle freely with strange chimpanzees and hold "carnivals" in the jungle moonlight. Most interspecies contacts, such as between baboons and chimpanzees or lemurs and langurs, are rather diffident, although chimpanzees have been known to catch and eat a young monkey.

According to the testimony of widely separated observers, coalitions are an important feature of social behavior in primate groups. The De Vore volume provides several examples.

A team of observers [6] studied groups of rhesus monkeys living comfortably on the grounds of a temple in the north Indian city of Aligarh. One of these groups, with a total population of forty, contained nine adult males. The observers learned to recognize the males individually and assigned each one a descriptive name such as Thigh-wound or Cleft Chin. Rhesus monkeys are moderately quarrelsome and the observers were able to determine the status order of the adult males by tabulating the results of aggressive encounters.

The "outcome of 119 two-male aggressive encounters" is shown in Table 4–1. Some of these disputes occurred naturally and some were deliberately provoked by an observer. The relationships together form nearly a "perfect hierarchy." [8] Only three encounters had an unexpected outcome, and all three involved Young Cut-lip, a low-ranking but ob-

---

[5] Although, according to Desmond Morris, the sexuality of baboons is negligible compared to that of humans. See his *The Naked Ape: A Zoologist's Study of the Human Animal* (London: Jonathan Cape, 1967), 62–63.

[6] Charles H. Southwick, Mirza Azhar Beg, and M. Rafiq Siddiq, "Rhesus Monkeys in North India," Chap. 4 in DeVore, *ibid.*, pp. 111–59.

[8] A hierarchy with completely consistent status relationships.

TABLE 4-1 [7]

Dominance Relationships of Adult Males in a Group of Rhesus Monkeys. Number of Aggressive Interactions with Dominance Expressed *

Dominance Rank: Highest to Lowest	Shifty	Fat-intact	Fat Cut-lip	Thigh-wound	White-face	Young Cut-lip	Cleft Chin	Blue Chest	Gray Cheek
Shifty		8	2	6	3	2		2	1
Fat-intact			3	3	2	2		1	2
Fat Cut-lip				5	4	2	1	1	1
Thigh-wound					8	5	6	3	2
Whiteface						2	1	3	7
Young Cut-lip					2		9	6	5
Cleft Chin						1		2	2
Blue Chest									4
Gray Cheek									

* The numerical tabulations represent the number of observed interactions in which the male in the vertical row on the left was dominant to the male in the horizontal top row.

[7] *Ibid.*, Table 4–10, p. 149.

viously ambitious monkey. According to the observers, the group normally moved in three sections. The first included Fat Cut-lip and Fat-intact, together with most of the females and their young. The second included Shifty, four females, and many juveniles and infants. The third, or bachelors', section included the remaining males. The group as a whole exhibited a fairly complex and sophisticated pattern of interaction; for example, low status in a high ranking section was exchangeable for high status in a low ranking section.

At the top of the monkey hierarchy there were three males, Shifty, Fat-intact, and Fat Cut-lip. Fat-intact was slightly dominant over Fat Cut-lip and Shifty dominated them both. They formed a Type 5 triad in a continuous situation and, sure enough, the predictable *BC* coalition appeared:

> In a direct aggressive conflict between "Shifty" and either of the fat males, "Shifty" was dominant. Both of the fat males together, however, were dominant to "Shifty." Aggressive conflict between the three males was relatively rare, however.[9]

The balance of power between Shifty and the stable *BC* coalition of Fat-intact and Fat Cut-lip helps to explain the separation of the females and young into two sections, the larger controlled by the coalition and the smaller by Shifty. The observers noted some transfer of females, infants, and juveniles between the two subgroups, but these individuals were more difficult to identify than the adult males and their movements could not be accurately recorded.

The leading section contained another important triad, this one of Type 3 with Fat-intact as *A* and Fat Cut-lip and Young Cut-lip as *B* and *C*. This triad was dominated by the conservative coalition *AB*, which was never challenged by Young Cut-lip:

> He was permitted to feed and rest in close proximity to them, but he was very subordinate to both. Antagonistic encounters were rare, possibly because of the wide dominance gap between them.[10]

However, Young Cut-lip's participation in the central triad enabled him to swagger mightily among the low ranking males of the third section. He dominated Whiteface in the presence of Fat-intact although he was dominated by Whiteface when they met alone.

Young Cut-lip's position as the monkey in the middle was reflected by his high rate of interaction with the monkeys of the bachelor section, with whom his superiors had very little to do. Occasionally, like many a staff officer, he exceeded his authority, and on two observed occasions

9 Southwick, *et al.,* p. 146.
10 *Ibid.,* p. 151.

he was attacked and put to rout by a three-way coalition of the lowest-ranking bachelors.

Another and more complicated hierarchy was observed by Hall and DeVore in a group of baboons in Nairobi Park.[11] Here, too, the outcome of aggressive encounters among adult males was tabulated, combining natural encounters and those provoked by an observer.[12] The enumeration (Table 4–2) was not restricted to pairs; it included encounters that

TABLE 4–2 [13]

Dominance Relationships of Adult Males in a Group of Baboons—Number of Encounters with Dominance Expressed

Dominating Baboon	Dano	Pua	Kula	Mdomo	Mark	Kovu	Total Dominance
Dano	–	8	9	4	7	3	31
Pua	5	–	1	6	2	7	21
Kula	4	5	–	6	6	3	24
Mdomo	3	4	5	–	1	11	24
Mark	–	4	–	–	–	4	8
Kovu	–	–	–	–	–	–	0
Total Submission	12	21	15	16	16	28	

involved coalitions or were affected by the presence of third parties. The six baboons were approximately equal in size but differed greatly in age and fitness. Kovu was very old, Pua was old, Dano and Mdomo were "late prime," Mark was "young prime," and Kula was "prime."

The hierarchy disclosed by Table 4–2 is somewhat irregular. Dano was clearly the leading animal, dominating more often and submitting less often than any of the others, but his dominance was statistical, not absolute. He was sometimes overawed by Pua, Kula, or Mdomo. Kovu, the very old baboon, never dominated anyone, but yielded gracefully to the comparative youth and vigor of the others. Mark was obviously still a recruit, occasionally dominating an elder but always deferring to baboons in their prime.

The pattern changes in a surprising way as soon as we take into account various coalitions and combinations. A sort of gerontocracy appears, in which

11 K. R. L. Hall and Irven DeVore, "Baboon Social Behavior," Chap. 3 in DeVore, *op. cit.*

12 Called "food incentive tests."

13 Adapted from Table 3–2, Hall and DeVore, *op. cit.*, p. 60, by combining experimental and natural situations.

. . . the three central hierarchy males (Dano, Pua, Kovu) not only combined against the other males, but also were very uncompetitive among themselves with regard to food. These three males would feed side by side when food was thrown to them. Although Kovu was obviously less assertive in these situations, Dano and Pua were never assertive toward each other over food. . . . They ordinarily acted in concert and together controlled access to incentives, determined group movement, and so on. In every instance where Dano, Pua and Kovu or Dano and Pua combined, they were 100 per cent successful against any of the other three males, who rarely combined.[14]

The influence of the ruling triad even extended to sexual opportunities in which equal sharing was not possible. This group was unique among those observed in having a shortage of females. There were only seven mature females for the six males and not all the females would be in estrus at the same time. The shortage led to fighting among the males and they harassed each other during copulation. According to the observers an adult male's dominance could be measured by the number of times he was able to copulate successfully with females in full estrus. Dano showed the highest score for completed copulations, but he was followed by the ancient and infirm Kovu. This

. . . illustrates how a male's position in the central hierarchy gives him an advantage over other adult males in mating activities. Kovu, an old male whose teeth were worn level with his gums and who was *individually* the least dominant adult male in the group, was nevertheless second only to the most dominant male in copulations completed at the time of maximum swelling in the female. Since ovulation occurs during the period of maximum swelling, it is likely that he was therefore one of the most effective breeders in the group.[15]

The same report describes another band of baboons in Nairobi Park ruled by a coalition. This group contained six adult males and about twice as many adult females. The three leading baboons were Curly, Humbert, and Gam, but Curly and Humbert formed a permanent coalition dominating Gam and all the others. Lone, a subordinate member of a neighboring band, began to frequent the fringes of the group. At first he fought viciously with Curly, who succeeded in forcing him to the edge of the group but could not drive him away. Then Humbert disappeared; the observers hint at foul play. Gam and Lone gradually developed a new coalition to which Curly and the other remaining males were subordinate.

Another triad containing a stable coalition was observed by Jane Goodall among chimpanzees of the Gombe Stream Reserve in Tanganyika.[16]

---

14 *Ibid.*, p. 61.
15 *Ibid.*, p. 76.
16 Jane Goodall, "Chimpanzees of the Gombe Stream Reserve," Chap. 12 in DeVore, *op. cit.*

Chimpanzees seem to have a looser and more flexible form of association than other apes and they are distinctly more suspicious of human intruders. It took ten months, averaging twelve hours a day in the field, before Miss Goodall could approach within 100 feet of the animals. After eighteen months three mature males became tame enough to take food from her hand, and she was able to observe their relationships in detail. She named them David Greybeard, Goliath, and William. Goliath was the largest and most powerful, William was weak and timid. Her report is brief but very illuminating:

> Data obtained from a close study of interrelationships between the three "tame" males, however, suggest that although one particular individual may always appear dominant to another over an indefinite period, its dominance status with regard to other individuals may change according to the situation. Thus David Greybeard was dominant over William in all interactions observed between the two; he was dominant over Goliath in all situations except when the latter became particularly excited, when David ran away from him screaming. Goliath was always dominant over William when David was present; when David was absent the other two appeared to rank as equals. This was apparently due to a greater degree of mutual attraction between Goliath and David (who was the dominant male of the three except on rare occasions).[17]

Here is the first animal case of a Type 2 triad [A > B, B = C, A < (B + C)] complete with the interesting nuance that David can ordinarily dominate his weaker coalition partner Goliath but is not always able to manage Goliath's emotions.

[17] *Ibid.,* p. 454.

ORGANIZATIONAL
TRIADS

An organizational triad is a triad whose members belong to an organization and are required by its program to interact with one another. These members may be either individuals or collectivities.

I have elsewhere defined an organization as a persistent social system with an explicit collective identity, an unequivocal roster of members, a program of repetitive activity directed towards the achievement of explicit goals, and procedures for the appointment of new members.[1] This definition includes organizations that vary greatly in size and purpose. Not only corporations and government bureaus are considered to be organizations, but also families, adolescent gangs, prisons and jails, workshops, ships' crews, theatrical companies, and religious sects.[2] It can be shown that every organization has a status order or hierarchy that arrays its members in order of their relative influence, so that when the organization requires them to interact, relationships of superiority, inferiority, and equality have been estab-

[1] *Principles of Organization* (New York: Harcourt, Brace & World, Inc., 1964), pp. 11–49.
[2] For an inclusive list of the kinds of organizations usually observable in the United States, see *ibid.*, pp. 48–49.

lished in advance and do not ordinarily require a trial of strength.

The concepts of organization and hierarchy are nearly inseparable. The skeleton of every organization is a *status order* and every fixed status order is embodied in an organization.

A live organization is composed of real people set in a framework of abstractions—relationships, procedures, and rules. Each *person*—unique, fragile, irreplaceable—occupies a *position* that carries a pattern of standardized activity with it. A great deal of behavior is successfully shaped by these patterns but unexpected deviations often occur. When we analyze an organizational triad, we must not confuse its status order, which represents expectations, with its power distribution, which represents actual behavior.

Discrepancies between the two arise from a number of causes. The aggressiveness of one member and the timidity of another may cause them to exercise more or less power in the same position. The history of the triad often makes a difference, for an individual's power is partly dependent on his success or failure in past coalition episodes. The power distribution is also affected by different intensities of involvement.

But the most important source of discrepancy between status and power is the coalition process itself. The numerous coalitions that convert weakness into strength or strength into weakness always threaten to upset the status order.

CONSERVATIVE, REVOLUTIONARY, AND IMPROPER COALITIONS

Consider, for example, an organizational triad whose status order identifies it as the familiar Type 5. A is entitled to control B and B is entitled to control C, but A's authority would not be effective against the combined resistance of B and C.

The most likely coalition in a triadic game would be BC, as pointed out in a previous chapter. However, if a BC coalition forms in this triad, the power distribution that should develop from the status order is upset. A, who was intended to be the most powerful member, is overthrown and replaced by B, who dominates A by means of the BC coalition and dominates C by virtue of his superiority within the coalition. BC is a *revolutionary coalition, which is a winning coalition that dominates the superior member of an organizational triad.*

The BC coalition is such a clear and present danger to A in an organizational triad of Type 5 that he will probably try to form an AB or AC coalition for his own protection. An AB coalition would leave the power distribution undisturbed. A would continue to dominate B and B would continue to dominate C just as the status order specifies although by slightly different means. AB is a *conservative coalition, which is a coalition that does not upset the prescribed status order in an organizational triad.*

The third possible coalition *AC* would preserve *A*'s superiority at the cost of creating an ambiguous relationship between *B* and *C*. *B* would continue to be stronger than *C* as an individual but could be dominated by *C* as a member of the *AC* coalition within which *C* is a junior partner. Neither *B* nor *C* could exercise power with any confidence and the triad might find it difficult to function at all. From the standpoint of the larger organization, the coalition *AC* is *improper* because the organization's representative *A* has undermined the legitimate authority of *B* over *C*. An *improper coalition in an organizational triad is a coalition that is not conservative or revolutionary.*

An organization is above all a mechanism for achieving definite goals, for getting things done that could not be done as well or at all by unorganized individuals. From the organization's viewpoint every member is an instrument for the accomplishment of collective tasks, and the status order, which stretches unbroken from the top to the bottom of the system, assigns responsibility for the use of each human instrument to his direct superiors.

OFFICIAL AND PRIVATE PROGRAMS

The organization is a mechanism but it is not a machine. Its essential working parts are human and differ greatly from inanimate instruments. To function at an acceptable level of efficiency, the human instrument must be "motivated," that is, he must want to do for his own sake what the organization wants him to do on its behalf. His own program must be consistent with the organization's program.

However, except under extreme conditions, the private program of an organization man never coincides exactly with the official program assigned to his position. The actions of men are always affected by a multitude of unconscious needs and by vestigial emotions developed earlier in life, and the members of a given organization usually belong to other organizations which have partly incompatible programs. Most important, transactions between an organization and its members embody a fundamental conflict of interest, the members wanting to maximize the rewards they receive for participating and the organization wanting to minimize the cost of their participation.

The inherent discrepancy between the collective interests of an organization and the personal interests of its members is usually resolved by an arrangement of graduated rewards whereby higher status members receive more pay, perquisites, and prestige in return for their organizational efforts than do lower status members. The intended result is that a superior dealing with subordinates will identify the preservation of his own advantages with the maintenance of the status order and with conformity to the official program.

Since superiors have other personal goals in addition to the defense of their privileges and their subordinates have independent reasons for wanting the organization to prosper, it sometimes happens that the official goals are pursued more vigorously by subordinates than by superiors. For instance, several studies have described factory workers who conspire against their supervisors in order to maintain efficient production.[3] But the normal expectation is the converse. The official program is inextricably bound up with the status order and its accomplishments seem to depend on keeping the status order intact, if only to provide a reliable channel for upward and downward communication. The essential condition for the continuation of the status order is that when a superior and a subordinate interact on organizational matters, the superior's greater power will enable him both to use the subordinate for the furtherance of the official program and to keep the subordinate's pursuit of his private program within tolerable limits.

A status order is a unified system. Metaphorically, it is a chain of command or a ladder of positions and like these objects it is useless if broken at any point. The organization anticipates that any superior faced with a rebellious subordinate will turn to his own superior for help. The refusal of help under these circumstances would signify either that the man in the middle had been eliminated from the hierarchy or that a segment of the organization had collapsed. The normal, expected alliance between two superiors against a subordinate is the conservative coalition, and it is presumably formed to support the official program and suppress private programs. The revolutionary coalition of two subordinates against a superior usually reflects the triumph of private programs over the official program.

The improper coalition, as we have seen, increases the power of one superior while undermining the equally legitimate power of another. It is a mixture of the two previous strategies and its significance must be deciphered according to the circumstances.

TYPES OF ORGANIZATIONAL TRIAD

The eight basic types of organizational triad [4] are the same types of triads described in earlier chapters. They may be classified initially by

[3] The classic study is Donald Roy's "Efficiency and 'the Fix': Informal Intergroup Relations in a Piecework Machine Shop," *American Journal of Sociology*, LX, No. 3 (November 1954), pp. 255–66.

[4] A different scheme for classifying organizational triads is proposed by James A. Davis and Samuel Leinhardt in a recent paper, "The Structure of Positive Interpersonal Relations in Small Groups," Dartmouth College, 1967 (mimeographed).

the number of status levels they contain. Type 1 triads have only a single level of equals. Types 2, 3, 4, and 8 are two-level triads, containing either a superior and two inferiors, or an inferior and two superiors. Types 5, 6, and 7 are three-level triads, containing no equals.

FIGURE 5–1

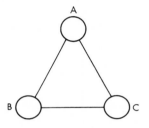

In the single-level triad, Type 1, *any* coalitions must be considered revolutionary. There are no conservative or improper coalitions. The probability that a coalition will be formed is high, and any member who is determined to keep himself aloof can be fairly certain that his two peers will be tempted by the advantages of a coalition against him.

In real life, absolute equality is a condition that is difficult to achieve or to bestow. Most organizational triads that seem to resemble Type 1 actually have one member who is notably stronger than the others.

FIGURE 5–2

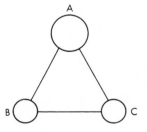

The Type 2 triad is inherently unstable. It contains a potential revolutionary coalition *BC* but no conservative coalition at all, both *AB* and *AC* being improper. The ordinary experience of administrators is consistent with the theory that deplores the situation of a superior faced by two equal subordinates whose combined power exceeds his own. Since *A* is greatly threatened by the potential *BC* coalition, he is likely to attempt to establish one of the improper coalitions on a permanent basis and thus convert the triad from Type 2 to Type 5.

FIGURE 5–3

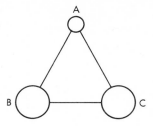

Type 3 triads may be either stable or unstable. Each of the superior members, *B* and *C,* can choose between a conservative coalition with an equal partner and a revolutionary coalition with the weaker *A.* This pattern obviously encourages maneuvering and intrigue, and is the only type of triad in which an organizational superior may prefer a revolutionary coalition that upsets the status order to a conservative coalition that would maintain it.

FIGURE 5–4

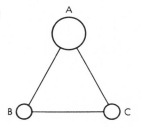

Revolutionary coalitions are impossible in Type 4 triads. A *BC* coalition of the equal inferiors is conservative. In simplified form it represents the peer-group pattern characteristic of large-scale organizations. In a normal organizational environment, there is little inducement for *A* to enter into one of the improper coalitions *AB* or *AC,* but *B* and *C* would gain considerable advantage by uniting, the difference in power between *A* and *BC* being less than the difference between *A* and *B* or *C* separately. Thus the motives for *B* and *C* to form a conservative coalition are self-evident, whereas special circumstances are needed to provoke the improper coalitions *AB* or *AC.*

In a Type 5 triad the coalition *BC* is revolutionary, enabling *B* to replace *A* as the dominant actor in the triad. The revolutionary coalition can be forestalled either by the conservative coalition *AB* or by the

FIGURE 5–5

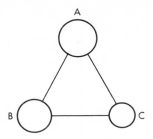

improper coalition *AC*. However, the minimum winning coalition would be expected to prevail, in the absence of external constraints.

FIGURE 5–6

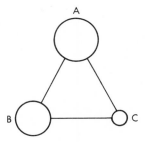

In a Type 6 triad, by contrast, there can be no revolutionary coalition, since no combination of *B* and *C* can disturb the dominance of *A*. *AC* remains improper, but both *AB* and *BC* are conservative. For reasons to be given later, we expect *B* to prefer the *AB* coalition given a choice between the two conservative coalitions.

In the Type 7 triad, there can be one conservative coalition *AB* and two improper coalitions, *BC* and *AC*. *BC* is improper because it blocks *A* without dominating him and establishes an impasse, but under certain circumstances, it may have the same effect as a revolutionary coalition.

FIGURE 5–7

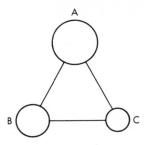

The Type 8 triad is an organizational monstrosity. All its coalitions are improper. *A* cannot form any coalition that will support the prescribed status order, and *B* and *C* have no hope of dominating *A*. The activity of the triad can be brought to a standstill by the improper coalition *BC,* or it may attempt to function under one of the improper coalitions *AB* or *AC.* If the attempt is successful, the triad will have been transformed into a Type 5 triad.

FIGURE 5–8

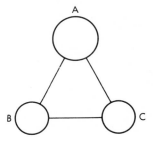

IMPLICATIONS OF REVOLUTIONARY COALITIONS

Table 5–1 summarizes the conservative, revolutionary, and improper coalitions in each of the eight basic types of triads. In the light of our previous discussion of triadic games, something unexpected appears.

It will be remembered from Chapter 3 that Gamson refined the original model for predicting coalitions in triadic games and identified the *cheapest winning coalition* as that most likely to be formed in all types of triads. His predictions are shown in Table 3–2.

Gamson's list of cheapest winning coalitions in triadic games is *identical* to our list of possible revolutionary coalitions in organizational triads. This startling convergence raises immediate questions. Do stable

TABLE 5–1

Conservative, Revolutionary, and Improper Coalitions in Organizational Triads

Type	Power Distribution	Conservative	Possible Coalitions Revolutionary	Improper
1	$A = B = C$	—	AB, BC, AC	—
2	$A > B$, $B = C$, $A < (B + C)$	—	BC	AB, AC
3	$A = B$, $B > C$	AB	AC, BC	—
4	$A > (B + C)$, $B = C$	BC	—	AB, AC
5	$A > B > C$, $A < (B + C)$	AB	BC	AC
6	$A > B > C$, $A > (B + C)$	AB, BC	—	AC
7	$A > B > C$, $A = (B + C)$	AB	—	BC, AC
8	$A = (B + C)$, $B = C$	—	—	AB, BC, AC

organizations somehow manage to avoid the triadic patterns in which revolutionary coalitions are possible? Or must we look for factors that make the formation of revolutionary coalitions less probable in organizational triads than in triadic games? The answer to *both* questions is yes. The designers of organizations usually try to avoid triads of Types 2 and 5, in which a superior can easily be dominated by his two immediate subordinates and the advantages of the revolutionary coalition are obvious to anyone. They are also suspicious of Type 3 triads, which offer a choice of two revolutionary coalitions to the subordinate confronting a pair of superiors, but triads of this type are difficult to avoid in a pyramidal organization that requires interaction between equals.

Other elements also inhibit the formation of revolutionary coalitions in organizational triads, for example, a *status schism* that forbids potential coalition partners to fraternize. In an infantry company led by a Type 5 triad composed of commanding officer, executive officer, and first sergeant, the status schism between officers and enlisted men will normally prevent a revolutionary coalition between the executive officer and the first sergeant.

Peer-group solidarity often has the same effect, although with less certainty. The members of a solidary peer group are discouraged from fraternizing with either superiors or inferiors. If either *B* or *C* in a triad of Type 5, or *C* in a triad of Type 3, is watched by jealous peers, revolutionary coalitions will be much less likely to form. On the other hand, in a Type 2 triad, the chance of a revolutionary coalition being formed is increased by peer-group solidarity.

In triads of Type 5 in which the choice between the conservative and the revolutionary coalition is always the responsibility of *B,* the man in the middle, an alert organization can devise threats and blandishments to entice him towards the conservative option. The literature that characterizes the industrial foreman as a marginal man, wavering between the roles of manager and worker, describes several managerial solutions to the problem.

EFFECTS OF LINKAGE

But the most important limitations on the formation of revolutionary coalitions in organizational hierarchies result from the coalition process itself. A hierarchy with more than three ranks can be visualized as a chain of linked triads. Within the chain, given the appropriate conditions, revolutionary coalitions are unexpectedly transformed into hierarchical strata.

FIGURE 5–9

A Chain of Type 5 Triads

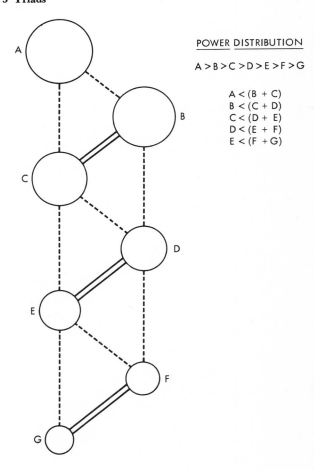

POWER DISTRIBUTION

$A > B > C > D > E > F > G$

$A < (B + C)$
$B < (C + D)$
$C < (D + E)$
$D < (E + F)$
$E < (F + G)$

A simple hierarchy with seven ranks is diagrammed in Figure 5–9. Since each superior is weaker than his two immediate subordinates combined, we have a chain of five linked Type 5 triads—*ABC, BCD, CDE, DEF,* and *EFG.*[5]

We will assume that the organization places no constraints on the formation of revolutionary coalitions—there are no rules of any kind against such coalitions and any member is free to join one when he is invited to do so. However, since the triads are linked, two additional principles must be introduced to make the model workable. First, *in a set of linked triads, a coalition partner in one triad may not be an opponent in another.*

When an actor is invited to join two potential coalitions, so situated that his partner, if he joined one coalition, would be his opponent if he joined the other coalition, the coalitions in question are *incompatible.* He must choose one (or neither), but he cannot choose both. In Figure 5–9, for example, *C* may join the revolutionary coalition *BC* in triad *ABC* or the revolutionary coalition *CD* in triad *BCD,* or neither, but he may not join both, since that would put *two* coalitions in the triad *BCD* and would require *C* to treat *B* simultaneously as a partner and as an opponent.[6]

Second, *in a set of linked triads, an actor who is offered a choice between incompatible winning coalitions will choose the winning coalition in the superior triad.* The reason for this may be seen by inspection of *C*'s position in Figure 5–9. Faced with a choice between *BC,* the winning coalition in triad *ABC,* and *CD,* the winning coalition in triad *BCD,* he might be tempted to choose *CD* because *within* that winning coalition he will be dominant, whereas if he chooses *BC,* the winning coalition in triad *BCD,* he will be dominated by his partner. "Better to be first in a little Iberian village," he might mutter, "than second in Rome" (but only, on reflection, if communications are poor between Rome and Iberia). If *C* joins the *CD* coalition and makes *B* his opponent in triad *BCD,* he inevitably makes *B* his opponent in triad *ABC* also, and in that triad, he is at *B*'s mercy. The same reasoning, we may suppose, will persuade *E* to choose the revolutionary coalition *DE* in triad *CDE* in preference to the equally victorious coalition *EF* in triad *DEF,* and this leaves *F* and *G* with no alternative but the coalition *FG.* As the diagram shows,

---

5 If all members of the hierarchy interact, there are other linked triads in the chain, such as *ACD* and *ADF*. Depending on the initial power distribution, these extra triads may be of Type 5 or Type 6. In this example, the linkage effects are not changed when the extra triads are taken into account.

6 Coalition partners in one situation are often opponents in another, but not within the same system of action. One's bridge partner may become one's opponent in tennis doubles, or even in the next rubber of bridge, but he must be unequivocally a partner *or* an opponent for the duration of each game.

the formation of these revolutionary coalitions, rather than disrupting the hierarchy, reorganizes it into three strata. There is still some trouble at the top of the system, where *A*'s authority is contravened by the revolutionary coalition *BC,* but this is not necessarily a problem for the organization as a whole and it can easily be remedied by increasing *A*'s power until the triad *ABC* is converted to a Type 6 triad. If the remainder of the power distribution is continued unchanged, a pattern of stratification again emerges from the coalition process, as shown in Figure 5–10. In this case, *C* is assumed to prefer *CD,* the winning revolutionary coalition in triad *BCD,* to *BC,* the nonwinning conservative coalition in triad *ABC.* The rest of the development proceeds as before.

FIGURE 5–10

A Chain of Type 5 Triads Headed by a Type 6 Triad

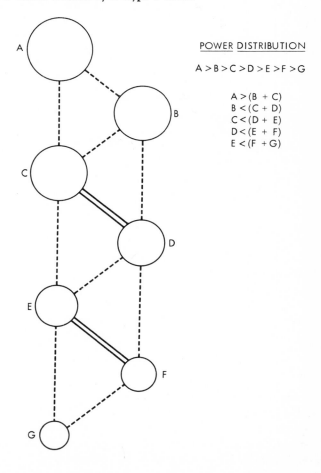

POWER DISTRIBUTION

A > B > C > D > E > F > G

A > (B + C)
B < (C + D)
C < (D + E)
D < (E + F)
E < (F + G)

These transformations illustrate how the revolutionary coalitions formed to seize power in superior triads become conservative coalitions, supporting the status order, in inferior triads. Thus, in Figure 5–9, although *CD* is a revolutionary coalition in triad *BCD*, it is a conservative nonwinning coalition in triad *ACD*, and a conservative winning coalition in triads *CDE*, *CDF*, and *CDG*.

In addition to Type 5 triads, revolutionary coalitions are possible in triads of Types 2 and 3. In a Type 2 triad, the two equal inferiors can combine to overthrow the superior. In a Type 3 triad, either of the two equal superiors can combine with the inferior to overthrow his colleague. But orderly stratification appears again if the principles of linkage introduced above are applied to a chain of Type 2 triads, as in Figure 5–11.

FIGURE 5–11

A Chain of Type 2 Triads

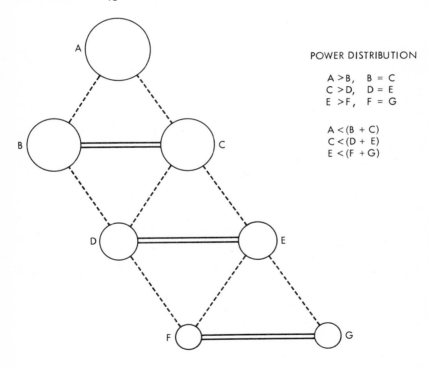

POWER DISTRIBUTION

A > B, B = C
C > D, D = E
E > F, F = G

A < (B + C)
C < (D + E)
E < (F + G)

This figure presents a condition very often encountered in modern bureaucracies in which the power of individual superiors is greatly limited, solidarity among peers is much greater than that between superiors and subordinates, and peers call on each other for help both in resisting authority and in coping with insubordination.

VI

THE
PRIMARY TRIAD

INTRODUCTION

Triads composed of parents and their children are the subject of the present chapter. Other family triads, such as the sibling triad and the classic constellation of father-son-mother's brother, will be considered in the next chapter.

The primary triad of father-mother-child takes various forms in different societies. There are a few societies in which the father-mother-child triad does not play a great part in the growing child's experience, either because the father is missing from the family, or because his usual responsibilities have been assigned to a male relative of the mother, or because child-rearing is a communal task. These cases are exceptional. The overwhelming majority of the human race, past and present, have awakened to consciousness in the presence of a pair of adults whom they called mother and father, by whom they were at first completely dominated, and from whom later, by slow degrees, they were emancipated.

Both the nuclear family and the extended family are organizations, as that term was defined above.[1] They have unequivocal

---

[1] Not all sociologists would agree with this. The usual objections are either that the family has no explicit goals, which seems absurd to me, or that it cannot replace *all* its members, which is true of many larger organizations as well.

collective identities, definite rosters of members, calendars of goal-directed activity, and procedures for appointing members—by marriage, birth-ceremonies, and adoption. The primary triad is an organizational triad and by necessity hierarchical. Like other organizational triads, it exhibits a visible tension between the official program imposed by superiors with the support of the larger social system and the private programs that individual members follow with whatever support they can muster. Both official and private programs have very wide scope in families. As the principal agency of socialization, the family transmits to its younger members not only the rules and regulations of family life but also the political, moral, religious, and esthetic norms of the larger communities to which the parents belong. As a consumer and producer cooperative, the family has a set of economic goals, and as a status-bearing unit it has complex strategies of achievement. The private programs in the family are extensive and embody fundamental differences of interest between male and female, young and old, the jealous and the contented.

As in other organizations, there is some disparity between means and ends in the family, and the procedures for reaching organizational goals are not always effective or efficient. The norms imposed on the family from outside do not necessarily form a perfectly harmonious whole. The vision of the world furnished by the local cosmology may hinder adaptation to reality. Some official programs are "dysfunctional" for the organization, and some private programs serve the collective goals better. Papa does not necessarily know best how to conserve the traditional values, let alone how to respond to innovations.

The analysis of the primary triad begins appropriately with its power distribution, that is, with a description or measurement of the power of each member in relation to each of the others at a given moment in time.

FORMATION OF THE PRIMARY TRIAD

It is difficult to fix the starting point. The new-born infant is not a social actor. He has no conscious goals and no ability to symbolize his instinctive wants, and he is not really qualified to enter into a coalition. But everything is prepared for him to become a social actor. At or near birth he is given a name and a position in the kinship structure that contains definite expectations about his future status. He is regarded from birth as a social being and "anthropomorphized" by the surrounding adults, who attribute social sentiments to him long before he can experience them directly. He arouses social reactions from the very beginning of his life and his presence often has as much catalytic effect on the interactions of other persons as if he were fully conscious. Mother and infant or even father and infant may form something that resembles a coalition before the infant learns to sit up.

The child emerges by slow degrees as an actor in his own right. The moment when the parental dyad is converted into a primary triad is not perceptible but it certainly occurs when the child is still small and very weak compared to either parent. He begins as an almost negligible *C* in a triad dominated by *A, B,* or an *AB* coalition. Then, if he is physically and mentally sound, his power will increase for many years until, depending on local customs, it approaches, equals, or surpasses the power of either parent. This shift in the power distribution, a source of instability in most family systems, is a distinctive feature of primary triads. Through the coalition process, the gradual increase in *C*'s power may have drastic effects on the relationship between his father and mother. In most societies, the relationship between spouses is not constant over time and is clearly affected by the changing power distribution within each primary triad as its filial member matures.

The norms that determine the relative power of spouses usually seem to allow for a good deal of individual variation. Although a husband has a higher status than his wife in an overwhelming majority of the primitive and historical societies that have been studied, henpecked husbands are found even in extremely patriarchal societies.[2]

There seems to be a general tendency (with many exceptions) for modernization to elevate the status of women. The family system in the United States is now usually described as egalitarian, but in other parts of the Western world it varies from egalitarian to mildly patriarchal. Statistical studies of power distribution in the modern family have been inconclusive, perhaps because they have relied on the report of a single family member.[3] Nevertheless, they do seem to show that many kinds of power distributions occur within the framework of the modern egalitarian family, including both full-fledged patriarchy and matriarchy.

CLASSIC FORMS OF THE PRIMARY TRIAD

Despite infinite variations in detail, three classic forms of the primary triad can be recognized. They are so widespread that they seem to be part of the basic repertory of human experience.

The Patripotestal Family. In this type of family, in which the domi-

---

[2] See, for example, Thomas Rhys Williams' description of husband-wife relationships in *The Dusun: A North Borneo Society* (New York: Holt, Rinehart & Winston, Inc., 1965).

[3] The most interesting of such studies is Charles E. Bowerman and Glen H. Elder, Jr., "Variations in Adolescent Perception of Family Power Structure," *American Sociological Review,* XXIX, No. 4 (August 1964), 551–67.

nance of the father cannot be challenged or overturned by any combination of wife and children, the primary triad is a triad of Type 6 with $A > B > C$ and $A > (B + C)$. The mother's domination of the child is less forceful than the father's, but it tends to persist as the child grows up. Although no revolutionary coalition is possible in such a family, mother and child have much to gain from a conservative BC coalition that welds them into a lifelong alliance to resist the father as much as they dare.

The patripotestal family is usually associated with open or covert polygamy together with intense male concern about the virtue of wives and daughters. The father's unquestioned power over the women of his family makes him responsible for their conduct. Moreover, in such families the possession of women is an important source of prestige that quickly turns into ridicule or dishonor if the possessor is unable to guard them from other men. Although the terms of virtue will be quite different for wives and daughters, paternal jealousy is equally quick to insist on virtue for both.

At the same time, the presence or threat of additional wives or mistresses, together with their children, competing for the father's property and favor imposes solidarity on the mother-child coalition. Rachel, plotting for her son Joseph to cheat Esau out of his birthright, was doing only what was expected of her. Esau was Jacob's first son by Leah, Rachel's older sister, and all those concerned, including the deluded patriarch, found Rachel's scheming too natural to be reprehensible.

The Equipotestal Family. For our present purposes, families in which husband and wife are essentially equal and those with mild paternal *or* maternal dominance form a single type in which either parent may be dominated by a coalition of the other parent with any child past infancy. In family systems characterized by mild paternal dominance, for example, the father dominates the mother or any child alone, but is unable to cope with a mother-child coalition. Families in such systems are often characterized by a kind of matriarchal drift—a tendency toward female domination as the children mature and the father's authority is increasingly checked by one or more revolutionary coalitions. The struggle for power may be gentle or furious and it may be carried out in a spirit ranging from high tragedy to low farce, so that situations of the same type often have quite dissimilar consequences. Variety and flexibility are characteristic of equipotestal family systems.

The Matripotestal Family. In a family of this type, the father does not generally acknowledge female authority but he belongs to the family only marginally and supports it only temporarily.[4] Our usual notation,

---

[4] The fullest description of such families may be found in Oscar Lewis, *La Vida* (New York: Random House, Inc., 1966). His subjects are a group of related, lower-class Puerto Rican families in San Juan and New York. See also Lee Rainwater, "Crucible of Identity: The Negro Lower-Class Family," *Daedalus*, XCV (1966), 172–216.

with the father as *A,* the mother as *B,* and the child as *C,* cannot be applied to the matripotestal family in which, at least in the long run, the mother is *A* and the father is not *B,* but *C*—a hanger-on whose permanent influence is less than the child's although he may dominate both mother and child during his occasional sojourns with them. In this case, the mother-child coalition has two aspects. While the father lives at home and supports the family, it is a revolutionary coalition that keeps him from asserting any decisive authority. In the longer run, it is a conservative coalition that prevents the father from interfering with the continuity of the household and permits the substitution of another man in his place without disturbance.

A HYPOTHETICAL HISTORY

The power distribution and the coalition pattern undergo many changes in the course of the family's life cycle. Let us follow a hypothetical American family through a typical sequence of power distributions, beginning with the birth of a son.

As noted above, the infant is not really a social actor, and we continue for a little while to see a dyad, in which father *A* dominates mother *B* in a mild fashion. When the child is about three years old, a triad begins to emerge, although the child's power is still negligible. The power distribution at this time is $A > B > C$, $A > (B + C)$, a triad of Type 6. A conservative *BC* coalition unites the mother and the son without challenging the father's domination.

But *C* continues to grow, increasing daily in size, strength, and influence. Since the difference in power between *A* and *B* was not very great to begin with, it will not be too long before *C*'s growth converts the triad to Type 7, the blocked hierarchy in which $A > B > C$, $A = (B + C)$. Eventually, the father can no longer dominate the primary triad alone, and for decisions to be made and goals to be pursued, *A* must form either a conservative coalition with *B* or an illegitimate coalition with *C*. If this is a normal family, there will probably be some experimentation with the *AC* coalition; father and son will explore common male interests like fishing or baseball. But it is difficult for father *A,* who spends his day away from home at work, to maintain a high rate of interaction with son *C,* who goes to school. As head of the family, *A* has little incentive to form a coalition that subverts the status order and invites conflict with his wife, and he is more likely to choose the parental coalition *AB* which is strong enough to dominate son *C* at this stage, and within which *A* will continue for a while to dominate his wife.

But only for a while. Son *C* continues to grow, and his power need not increase sharply to destroy the precarious balance of $A = (B + C)$. Quite soon we see the family transformed into a democratic hierarchy of

Type 5, in which $A > B > C$, but $A < (B + C)$. Any coalition is winning, but the improper coalition *AC* is unlikely. Father *A* has the same reasons to avoid it as before. Son *C*, quite aside from any oedipal preference for his mother, knows he will enjoy more influence in the mother-son coalition *BC* than in the father-son coalition *AC*. The two remaining possibilities, *AB* and *BC*, depend upon the choice of mother *B*. She need not be a profound strategist to perceive the advantage of the revolutionary coalition *BC* which would enable her to dominate father *A* by means of the coalition and son *C* within the coalition. Other things being equal (among other things, *C* being an only child), *BC* is the expected coalition and father *A* will no longer rule the roost.

But this is not the end of the story. *C* continues to grow, and the day comes when his unaided power is equal to his mother's. Once more the triad is transformed, this time to the troika form of Type 2, in which $A > B$, $B = C$, $A < (B + C)$.

In this new situation, the revolutionary coalition of mother and son can still dominate the father but with a significant change: within the coalition *BC* the mother is merely equal to the son and she faces a future in which she may gradually become the weaker member. It would not be surprising if at this point she began to reconsider the attractions of an *AB* coalition with the father which could dominate the son until he leaves the parental household.

We do not know if this is statistically the most frequent sequence of coalitions, but we know that all of the events in the sequence do occur in real life. How often, under what conditions, and with what variations they occur remain to be determined.

Even this intensely simplified version of a family history compels us to examine two complications that arise inevitably in the analysis of family triads.

LIKE AND UNLIKE COALITIONS

In the first place *all* primary triads (father-mother-child) are composed of two actors of one sex and one actor of the other sex. A triad has the inanely obvious property that if its members differ with respect to any quality, there must be two actors of one kind and one actor of another kind. It follows that all coalitions in such triads will then fall into two categories: (a) coalitions of like partners against an unlike opponent and (b) coalitions of unlike partners against an opponent who is like one of the partners. Since persons who share a socially meaningful quality necessarily have common interests, a coalition of unlike partners always has some flavor of betrayal, however slight. Given a constant power distribution, a coalition of like partners is usually a little easier to arrange. Thus, in family systems in which sons and daughters are approximately equal in power and symmetrical in their relationships to parents, we would expect to find that mother-daughter coalitions would be more durable than mother-son coalitions. In the same systems, coalitions of two brothers against a sister or two sisters against a brother ought to occur much more frequently than brother-sister coalitions.

Gender is never the only quality by which family members are significantly differentiated. Two generations are represented in every primary triad and, in that respect, a parental coalition is a coalition of like partners and a parent-child coalition, of unlike partners.

In many societies the members of a primary triad will belong to two different kinship categories, for example, in a moiety system in which the father and his children always belong to one group and their mother belongs to another. In our own society occupational differentiation crosscuts the primary triad in a curious way. Fathers and sons are likely to follow different occupations, whereas mothers and daughters are likely to share the universal female occupation of housewife, whether or not they have other employment.

There are even a fair number of societies in which father, mother, and child do not necessarily belong to the same social class, and in a few peculiar systems, they *cannot* all belong to the same class.[5]

All of these differences are significant. In particular, the ease with which like partners form coalitions and the uneasiness of coalitions between unlike partners may sharply modify the coalition expectation derived from the power distribution alone. In effect, we must add another dimension to the model in order to do justice to the complexities observed in real life.

Another significant implication of the principle that like partners are preferred to unlike partners is that coalitions are seldom completely fixed in the primary triad, since all primary triads are crosscut in such a way that partners alike in gender must necessarily belong to different generations and as noted above, the crosscutting does not necessarily end with gender and generation, but may extend to other important characteristics. Thus, although a given coalition may predominate on the basis of some balance of power and likeness, other coalitions will appear in the same primary triad in response to occasions that emphasize other kinds of likeness and unlikeness.[6] For example, in a patriarchal

[5] See the extraordinary marriage and descent system of the Natchez Indians as described by Kingsley Davis, "Intermarriage in Caste Societies," in Rose Laub Coser, ed., *The Family: Its Structure and Functions* (New York: St. Martins Press, Inc., 1964).

[6] Such fluctuation can be observed even in brief experimental sessions with family triads. See Fred L. Strodtbeck, "The Family as a Three-Person Group," *American Sociological Review*, XIX (1954), 23–29; and John F. O'Rourke, "Field and Laboratory: The Decision-Making Behavior of Family Groups in Two Experimental Conditions," *Sociometry*, XXVI, No. 4 (December 1963), 422–35.

family in which the mother-son coalition is generally salient, there may be religious occasions that elicit a father-son coalition because the religious duties of men and women are sharply differentiated, or there may be a property arrangement that elicits a parental coalition because the interests of parents and children are opposed.

This alternation of coalitions accounts for much of the vitality of family life and, under favorable conditions, it may contribute to the cohesiveness of the total family by preventing any single coalition from becoming too divisive. It is also, needless to say, a source of perennial instability and tension.

THE CHOICE OF COALITION PARTNERS
IN THE NUCLEAR FAMILY

Linked to a primary triad of father-mother-son there will be other triads such as father-mother-daughter, mother-son-daughter and father-mother-grandmother. A household of moderate size may contain more than a score of important and intimate triads. In all such networks there appear to be strong inclinations towards compatible coalitions.

In order to visualize how members of a family resolve the dilemma posed by incompatible coalition opportunities within the interlocking and overlapping triads of the nuclear family, we must again turn to a hypothetical family and consider its coalition process under a set of fixed assumptions.

The first pair of assumptions we have dealt with before while discussing a general model for linked organizational triads:

> In a set of linked triads a coalition partner in one triad may not be an opponent in another.
> In a set of linked triads an actor offered a choice between incompatible winning coalitions will choose the winning coalition in the superior triad.

Three additional assumptions are necessary to resolve all possible choices:

> The coalition partner selected for a winning coalition in one triad will be selected again by the same chooser whenever that partner is available to form a winning coalition in a linked triad.
> The superior member of a hierarchical triad will prefer a conservative winning coalition to an improper winning coalition.
> A winning coalition in an inferior triad will be preferred to an incompatible nonwinning coalition in a superior triad.

All of this sounds more abstruse than it is, and may be readily visualized by means of a simple example. Consider a nuclear family with mild paternal and parental dominance, consisting of father *A,* mother *B,* adolescent son *C,* and adolescent daughter *D.* The power distribution follows the order A > B > C > D, but A < (C + D), and also, of course, B < (C + D). Since the children combined are stronger than either parent alone, they must be of at least adolescent age.[7]

Figures 6–1 and 6–2 show two different coalition patterns that might occur in a family of this type under the assumptions listed above. The superior triad *ABC,* consisting of father, mother, and son, may be dominated either by a conservative *AB* coalition between the parents or by a revolutionary *BC* coalition between mother and son. The improper coalition *AC* is not an alternative because, under our assumptions, *A* would always prefer the conservative coalition *AB.* The chooser in this triad is the mother, who is offered either winning coalition *AB* or *BC.* The figure shows the implications of her choice.

FIGURE 6–1

A Conservative Coalition Pattern in a Four-Person Nuclear Family

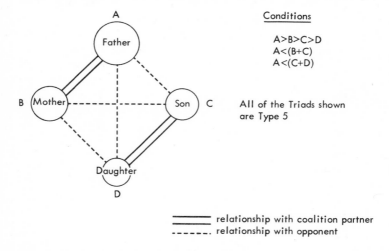

Conditions

A>B>C>D
A<(B+C)
A<(C+D)

All of the Triads shown
are Type 5

════════ relationship with coalition partner
▬ ▬ ▬ ▬ ▬. relationship with opponent

If she elects the parental coalition *AB,* the conservative pattern shown in Figure 6–1 follows. The parental coalition dominates the triads *ABC* and *ABD,* and the parents together dominate either child without difficulty. The triad *ACD* is dominated by a *CD* coalition, and this is the only coalition that can form in that triad under the "rule" that an

---

[7] This is only one of many possible power distributions for a four-person nuclear family composed of father, mother, son, and daughter, and it may even be rather unusual. There is no reason why the same principles could not be illustrated with a different power distribution. The whole point of triad theory is that different configurations of power lead to different outcomes.

FIGURE 6–2

A Revolutionary Coalition Pattern in a Four-Person Nuclear Family

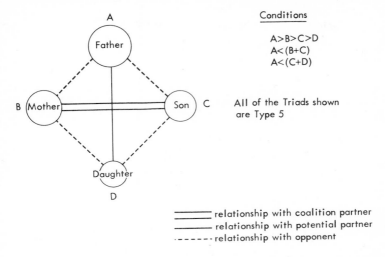

Conditions

A>B>C>D
A<(B+C)
A<(C+D)

All of the Triads shown
are Type 5

================ relationship with coalition partner
———————— relationship with potential partner
·— — — — — · relationship with opponent

opponent in one triad cannot become a partner in another. The triad
BCD will be dominated by the same *CD* coalition. Thus, neither parent
alone can dominate both children at the same time although either
parent dominates either child alone.

The pattern shown in Figure 6–2 illustrates what follows under our
assumptions if *B* chooses *BC,* the other winning coalition open to her
in the superior triad. The revolutionary coalition *BC* will dominate
both the superior triad *ABC* and the inferior triad *BCD,* that is, the
"oedipal" coalition of mother and son will dominate the father, although he is stronger than either of them alone, and the same coalition
will dominate the daughter in the inferior triad *BCD,* although this
represents no gain in power for the coalition partners, since either of
them can dominate her unaided. The daughter may be expected to seek
a coalition with the father, but as the figure shows, the father has no
reason to join an *AD* coalition: it would not enable him to dominate
the *BC* coalition of mother and son together and he can already dominate them alone.

As the number of persons in a nuclear family or other small network
increases, the potential coalitions soon become too numerous to analyze,
but some of the complexity is more apparent than real. The strain towards compatibility in the formation of coalitions is so strong that the
pattern of alliances and opposition within a network is largely determined by the coalitions that occur in one or two superior triads. Figures
6–3 and 6–4 show possible coalition patterns in a five-member nuclear

FIGURE 6–3

A Conservative Coalition Pattern in a Five-Person Nuclear Family

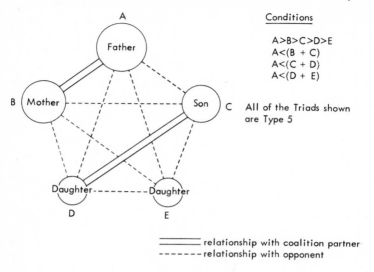

Conditions

A>B>C>D>E
A<(B + C)
A<(C + D)
A<(D + E)

All of the Triads shown
are Type 5

————— relationship with coalition partner
– – – – – relationship with opponent

FIGURE 6–4

A Revolutionary Coalition Pattern in a Five-Person Nuclear Family

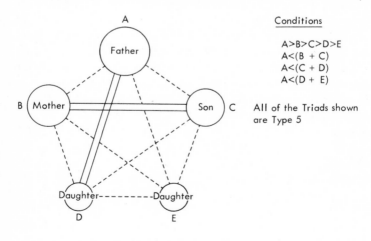

Conditions

A>B>C>D>E
A<(B + C)
A<(C + D)
A<(D + E)

All of the Triads shown
are Type 5

————— relationship with coalition partner
– – – – – relationship with opponent

family composed of father, mother, a son, and two daughters. As in the previous case, the mother *B* has a free choice between the conservative parental coalition *AB* and the revolutionary mother-son coalition *BC*. The power distribution has again been arranged so that every possible triad is of Type 5, including the inferior triad *CDE* composed of the three children. In the new triad *CDE, D* the elder daughter is the chooser and she will prefer the coalition *CD* with her brother because it can win in triads that are superior to *CDE*. The only change in the coalition pattern caused by the addition of the second daughter *E* is that the *CD* coalition, which, in the four-member family, was always revolu-tionary (in triads *ACD* and *BCD*), has now become a conservative win-ning coalition as well (in triad *CDE*).

The addition of the younger daughter would have considerably more effect on a family headed by a revolutionary coalition. In the four-member version of this family the father has no motive to form a coali-tion with his daughter *D*, but when the younger daughter is added and he faces the threat of domination by a *DE* coalition of the two girls we expect him quickly to enter an *AD* coalition. Under our assumptions, daughter *D* will prefer this *AD* coalition to the tempting revolutionary coalition of *DE* because *AD* dominates the superior, primary triad of *ABD*.

SOLIDARY TRIADS

The last two figures call attention to another possibility to which we have so far paid little attention: the *solidary* or three-way coalition. Like the triad with one coalition, the solidary triad is *balanced*,[8] mean-ing that its structure is stable because it does not violate the universal expectations that my friend's friend is my friend, my friend's enemy is my enemy, my enemy's friend is my enemy and my enemy's enemy is my friend. Solidary triads are not likely to develop when the stakes are high or when the option of a winning coalition is open. But they are very likely to appear in the inferior triad of a network. For example, in Figure 6–3 the addition of *E* to the sibling coalition *CD* would not be at all unusual—particularly if the combined power of the three-way coalition *CDE* equals or approaches that of the parental coalition *AB*. The *CD* coalition in the pattern shown loses very little when it accepts

[8] "A triad is balanced when all three of the relations are positive or when two of the relations are negative and one is positive"—Fritz Heider, *The Psychology of Inter-personal Relations* (New York: John Wiley & Sons, Inc., 1958), p. 202. For empirical evidence in support of balance theory, see Theodore M. Newcomb, *The Acquaintance Process* (New York: Holt, Rinehart and Winston, Inc., 1961) and Robert F. Priest & Jack Sawyer, "Proximity and Peership: Bases of Balance in Interpersonal Attraction," *American Journal of Sociology*, Vol. 72, No. 6 (May 1967), 633–49.

E as a partner instead of an opponent, since within the solidary triad *E* is still dominated by both her older brother and her older sister. The resulting pattern is shown in Figure 6–5. The incorporation of *C* prevents

FIGURE 6–5

Development of a Solidary Triad in a Five-Person Nuclear Family Headed by a Parental Coalition

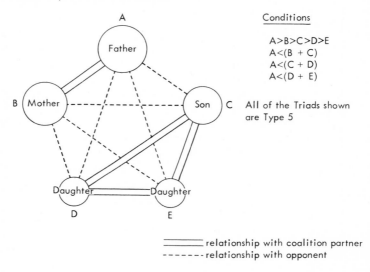

Conditions

$A>B>C>D>E$
$A<(B + C)$
$A<(C + D)$
$A<(D + E)$

All of the Triads shown are Type 5

========= relationship with coalition partner
- - - - - - relationship with opponent

her from indulging in any *tertius gaudens* maneuvers between the previously existing coalitions or between her parents and her older siblings.

NONWINNING COALITIONS IN THE PATRIARCHAL FAMILY

We have so far been discussing egalitarian or nearly egalitarian families in which ultimate control is determined by the outcome of the coalition process. Nonwinning coalitions also play a significant part in family life, especially in patriarchal family systems in which the father's authority over his wife and adolescent children enables him to rule without the aid of a coalition and without any apprehension that a winning coalition can be formed against him.

Among the Kgatla of Bechuanaland,[9] whose family system has been perceptively described by Schapera, the father's power over his wife and

---

[9] I. Schapera, *Married Life in an African Tribe* (Evanston: Northwestern University Press, 1966). A very similar coalition pattern is reported among the Nuer by E. E. Evans-Pritchard, *Kinship and Marriage Among the Nuer* (Oxford: Clarendon Press, 1951).

children is extreme, although lately it has been somewhat curbed by missionaries, administrators, and other outside authorities. The system is explicitly polygynous; women are legally and socially inferior to men and by Kgatla law are treated as minors. The sexes are traditionally segregated in everyday activities: the women, girls, and younger children at home, the men and older boys at the cattle posts. All family relationships are under the close scrutiny of a closeknit group of neighbors and kin.

The nonwinning conservative coalitions that normally appear in the Kgatla family when the children are adolescent are father-son and mother-daughter.

As the children grow older and begin to work, there develops a differentiation of authority, best summarized in the saying: "A boy takes his law from the councilplace" (i.e., from his father), "a girl takes her law from the compound" (i.e., from her mother). Girls are always at home with their mother until they are married. They work together with her, and most of their domestic education comes from her. They are generally on better terms, with her than with their father, and she is often their guide and confidante in matters of love. Boys after they go to the cattle-post are freed to a considerable extent from the control of their mother. Their work now brings them into much closer association with their father, whom they come to know more intimately and to appreciate. They learn from him the behaviour expected of men, and must always be ready to please him. They are apt at this stage to be rather scornful of their mother, and when at home seldom show her due respect or obedience, except when the father is about.[10]

Another type of patriarchal family is found in contemporary Brazil.[11] The husband's position in the Brazilian family is dominant and privileged. The wife is virtually a servant whom the husband is not obligated to help with housekeeping or child rearing. She is expected to be deferential and passive and strictly faithful, while the husband is quite free to engage in extramarital amours.

Children are taught to be submissive to *both* parents. The mother tyrannizes them through childhood and adolescence and even later. According to Rosen, it is not unusual for a mother to beat an adult son who has offended her.

The typical family pattern includes a conservative, nonwinning mother-son coalition within which the mother is protective, indulgent, highly involved, and dominant.

10 Schapera, *ibid.,* pp. 252–53.
11 As reported by Bernard C. Rosen, "Socialization and Achievement Motivation in Brazil," *American Sociological Review,* XXVII, No. 5 (October 1962), 612–24. See also Emilio Willems, "The Structure of the Brazilian Family," *Social Forces,* XXXI (May 1953).

In the Irish peasant families studied by Arensberg and Kimball [12] the father has a controlling role in all family activities, but he supervises his children directly only in the work on the farm. Most domestic matters are left to the wife, although the father serves as a court of last resort, whose punishments may be severe. The relationships between fathers and young adult sons are formal, constrained, and markedly ambivalent.

The mother is the constant companion of children of either sex throughout their earlier years, and she supports them emotionally throughout life. A mother-son coalition that partly protects the son against his father's authority is the usual outcome. The son "becomes confirmed, it is true, in a masculine scorn for feminine interests and pursuits, but he can and must still look for protection to his mother against a too-arbitrary exercise of his father's power. In family disputes the mother takes a diplomatic, conciliatory role." [13]

Thus, slight variations in these three patriarchal family systems lead to quite different coalition patterns. Among the Kgatla, a father-son coalition within which the father is moderately dominant opposes a mother-daughter coalition within which the mother is moderately dominant. In Brazil the mother-son coalition isolates the father without successfully challenging his authority and the mother is highly dominant within the mother-son coalition. In the Irish farm family the conservative mother-son coalition provides the son with an effective defense against the father's authority.

Can these outcomes be explained by power distributions alone? Undoubtedly not. Each of the three systems has its own set of cultural norms for viewing and regulating family relationships.

Among the Kgatla, men are held so much more valuable than women that even an adolescent son cannot be dominated by any woman or female coalition. There is no way he can threaten his father's authority, which is based on both law and custom and supported by the surrounding community. He and his father have considerable need of each other in dealing with the community and in protecting their common interests.

In Brazil, the son has no chance of successfully opposing either parent. His mother dominates him as completely as she is dominated by his father, and neither of them can shake off that control without leaving the family. Departure is not actually precluded, however, and the father is faced with two challenges that make him uneasy and irritable: the threat of the son's departure and the increasing difficulty he experiences in dealing with the mother-son coalition as the son matures. The characteristic domestic arrangements, with the mother continuously at home

---

[12] Conrad Arensberg and Solon T. Kimball, *Family and Community in Ireland* (Cambridge, Mass.: Harvard University Press, 1940).
[13] *Ibid.*, p. 59..

and the father rather remote from the household, make it difficult for the father to form coalitions with any of his children.

In the Irish farm family the relationship between mother and grown son approaches equality. After some years of service to the father the son may take over the direction of the family farm while his father sulks in helpless retirement, or he may seek his fortune elsewhere. In either case, he can look forward confidently to a day when he will no longer be subject to paternal authority, and there is nothing the father can do to prevent his eventual emancipation. The mother, however, enjoys a control of the household that she will not have to surrender even in her old age, for the growing up of her sons and the arrival of daughters-in-law will only strengthen her in relation to her husband. The mother-son coalition in this case is conservative and nonwinning, but bides its time.

OBJECTIONS AND QUALIFICATIONS

It may not be fanciful to hope that situations as complex as these can be understood by comparing their power distributions at various stages. Yet there is something repugnant about any theory of social behavior that insists on explaining too much with too little. There is much more to the interaction network of a nuclear family than to a game of pachisi, and a number of objections to this simplified view of the nuclear family immediately suggest themselves. Some of them can be met by further explanation of how the triadic model works or is supposed to work; others are not easy to answer.

One could object that the theory of coalitions concerns conflict but that the family is essentially cooperative. A model that dealt only with confrontations of power might well be judged incomplete. But nothing could be further from the case with regard to triad theory. The opposition between a coalition and its opponent is one side of a coin whose other side is solidarity.[14] Coalitions usually display mutual affection and loyalty. Each member seeks to interact with the other somewhat more than he needs to; each recognizes an obligation to protect the ego, the interests and the reputation of the other. Over and above the attachment of husband and wife, or of mother and son, a sentiment that resembles friendship develops in the presence of an opponent. Love and hate are both

---

14 One recent study of interaction in primary triads composed of a schizophrenic patient and his parents reports that the members of such a triad are unable to form coalitions either among themselves or with outsiders, and relates this inability to the pathogenic character of their interaction, which follows a "rule" that communications are habitually disaffirmed by senders and receivers. These findings are highly relevant to our discussion here. See Jay Haley, "The Family of the Schizophrenic: A Model System," in Gerald Handel, ed., *The Psychosocial Interior of the Family: A Sourcebook for the Study of Whole Families* (Chicago: Aldine Publishing Company, 1967).

coalition phenomena. Love is an intense preference for a particular coalition partner. Hate is an intense reaction against an opponent.

Family life is fraught with the tension of conflicting emotions precisely because it is based on coalitions and every coalition involves an opponent. Begun with a husband-wife coalition, continued by a mother-child coalition, and elaborated, in accordance with local custom, by mother-son, father-daughter, brother-brother, uncle-nephew, and other alliances, a family is sustained by the interlocking forces of love and hate in somewhat the same way that buildings are held up by the opposing forces of tension and compression.

In any particular family some coalitions may be culturally determined while others are freely chosen. The simplified model of the family network presented earlier in this chapter assigns equal probability to all coalitions, but in real life we observe that a family formed according to a given institutional model has a built-in tendency to form certain coalitions and to avoid others. Coalition constraints, like the well-known rule of mother-in-law avoidance, and coalition expectations, like the partiality of grandparents for grandchildren, are included in every cultural model.

THE NECESSITY OF AMBIVALENCE

Ambivalence in family interaction has been admirably described by Kirkpatrick, particularly as it occurs between parents and young children. It also occurs between spouses, siblings, and other familial pairs.[15] There have been practically no empirical studies of ambivalence, but incidental evidence suggests that it varies with differences of power and is more conspicuously exhibited by the dominated member of a pair. Unlike love and hate, liking and disliking, or affection and hostility, which tend to be mutual, ambivalence need not be reciprocated.

A typical victim of ambivalence is the son involved in a close coalition with his mother against a dominant father. If, as we surmise, ambivalence is an emotional strain that arises from interaction with someone who is both an opponent and a coalition partner, the reason for ambivalence in this simple case is obvious. No matter how solidary the mother-son coalition may be, there are circumstances in every family system that call for an automatic coalition of males. On some occasions the son must identify with the father and cooperate with him in a male activity from which the mother is excluded. Willy-nilly, the son must accept the father as a

15 Clifford Kirkpatrick, *The Family as Process and Institution* (2nd ed.) (New York: The Ronald Press Company, 1963), pp. 239 ff.

coalition partner part of the time while remaining in coalition with his mother. The father, although he may be annoyed or confused, is not subject to the same strain of attempting to maintain two incompatible coalitions at the same time.

Ambivalence, so viewed, can be defined geometrically. We have already noted that triads with three positive relationships, or with one positive and two negative relationships, are balanced, being special cases of a theory applicable to interaction networks of any size.[16] A triad with one negative and two positive relationships is unbalanced, and the pressure towards balance will be felt chiefly by the member involved in both positive relationships. Each of his incompatible coalition partners wants him to treat the other as an opponent, not as a partner. The pressure is greater if, as in the example above, he is the dominated member of both coalitions.

Carrying the principle a little further, we can see why ambivalence is a salient feature of most of the family systems that have been observed. A family begins with a parental coalition, and even if its solidarity later declines, that coalition must be revived from time to time in order to cope with emergencies. But the coalition of mother and child is perhaps the fundamental form of human relationship, and thus, though it is weakened as the child matures, it is seldom completely abrogated. The division of labor and the division of sex roles call forth occasions that require coalitions of males against a female or vice versa. The parental coalition is incompatible with both mother-child and same-sex coalitions. A mother-son coalition is incompatible with a father-son coalition.

The few family systems that do *not* display ambivalence are exceptions that clarify the underlying principles. At one extreme is the often cited (and perhaps partly imaginary) family system of the Nayar,[17] who carry matrilinearity to the point where the father is excluded from the nuclear family, and the Puerto Rican prostitutes studied by Lewis,[18] whose husbands are temporary and short-term. Lacking a father, these families do not develop parental coalitions or father-son coalitions. Among Lewis' subjects, some, but not much, ambivalence is elicited by stepfather and father substitutes. At the other extreme are family systems so patriarchal that mothers are outranked by their adolescent sons. These systems do not display much ambivalence, for the value of females as coalition partners is so low that they are never chosen in preference

16 See Fritz Heider, "Attitudes and Cognitive Organization," *Journal of Psychology,* XXI (January 1946), 107–12.

17 Most recently described by E. Kathleen Gough, "The Nayars and the Definition of Marriage," *Journal of the Royal Anthropological Institute,* LXXXIX (1959), 23–34.

18 Lewis, *op. cit.*

to a male and therefore no strain ensues. In effect, these extreme cases suggest that the problem of ambivalence in the nuclear family can only be resolved by changing the nuclear family into something else.

Societies do not simply accept this dilemma. They evolve complicated devices for removing some sources of ambivalence—at the price, perhaps, of reinforcing others. For example, in a matrilineal system like that of the Trobrianders,[19] the transfer of parental authority to the mother's brother frees the son from ambivalence towards his father. At the same time, a strong element of ambivalence is introduced into sibling relationships, especially between brothers.

Of course, there are other ways of interpreting the incompatibility of the fundamental coalitions in the family. On the one hand, following Freud and the Freudians, one may view coalition formation as a libidinal process which begins in infancy and continues through the sexual transformations of the maturing individual, without paying much attention to power distributions and their consequences. Or, following Parsons and Bales, one may view role differentiation, rather than dominance, as the critical feature of family networks. Beginning with a Freudian view of development, Parsons analyzes the transformation of the family by examining the differing motives of fathers and mothers, the specialization of fathers in instrumental, and mothers in expressive, functions, and the differential impact of these roles on their sons and daughters in the course of socialization.

FREUD'S THEORY OF FAMILY COALITIONS

Freud, that kindly and reasonable man, launched the oedipus complex in a letter to a friend in 1897:

> Being entirely honest with oneself is a good exercise. Only one idea of general value has occurred to me. I have found love of the mother and jealousy of the father in my own case too, and now believe it to be a general phenomenon of early childhood, even if it does not always occur so early as in children who have been made hysterics. (Similarly with the "romanticization of origins" in the case of paranoiacs—heroes, founders of religion.) If that is the case, the gripping power of *Oedipus Rex,* in spite of all the rational objections to the inexorable fate that the story presupposes, becomes intelligible, and one can understand why later fate dramas were such failures. Our feelings rise against any arbitrary, individual fate such as shown in the

[19] For example, see the works of Bronislaw Malinowski, esp. *The Father in Primitive Psychology* (New York: W. W. Norton & Company, Inc., 1927). For a very thorough discussion of this point, see Donald T. Campbell, "The Mutual Methodological Relevance of Anthropology and Sociology," in Francis L. K. Hsu, ed., *Psychological Anthropology* (Homewood, Ill.: Richard D. Irwin, Inc., 1961).

Ahnfrau, etc., but the Greek myth seizes on a compulsion which everyone recognizes because he has felt traces of it in himself. Every member of the audience was once a budding Oedipus in phantasy, and this dream-fulfillment played out in reality causes everyone to recoil in horror, with the full measure of repression which separates his infantile from his present state.[20]

In *The Interpretation of Dreams*,[21] written shortly after, he called attention to the common occurrence of dreams about the death of loved relatives and connected these dreams with childhood wishes, illustrating the hostility of small children to their brothers and sisters and of older children to new arrivals with anecdotes from his own family and practice. He then discussed dreams about the death of parents, insisting on his observation that men generally dream of their father's death and women of their mother's, and cited examples from Greek myths and the plays of Ibsen. He went on to say that the analysis of psychoneurotics shows that a girl's earliest affection is for her father and a boy's first childish desires are for his mother, so that each child has a rival in his parent of the same sex. He saw a "natural predilection" for father-daughter and mother-son coalitions:

> A natural predilection usually sees to it that a man tends to spoil his little daughters, while his wife takes her sons' part; though both of them, where their judgment is not disturbed by the magic of sex, keep a strict eye upon their children's education. The child is very well aware of this partiality and turns against that one of his parents who is opposed to showing it. Being loved by an adult does not merely bring a child the satisfaction of a special need; it also means that he will get what he wants in every other respect as well. Thus he will be following his own sexual instinct and at the same time giving fresh strength to the inclination shown by his parents if his choice between them falls in with theirs.[22]

Freud found the universality of this pattern confirmed by his domestic experience, by the reports of his patients, and also by his reading. He claims that the *Oedipus Rex* of Sophocles has a special effect on modern audiences because we recognize that Oedipus' destiny might have been ours. The "same curse" has been laid upon us "to direct our first sexual impulse towards our mother and our first hatred and our first murderous wish against our father." The structure of the play, with its gradual, exciting revelation of a secret buried in the past, is compared to psychoanalysis, and Freud finds indications in the text that the legend sprang

20 Sigmund Freud, *The Origins of Psycho-Analysis*, trans. Eric Masbacher and James Strachey (New York: Basic Books, Inc., Publishers, 1954), pp. 223–24.

21 Sigmund Freud, *The Interpretation of Dreams*, trans. James Strachey (London: The Hogarth Press, Ltd., 1958), pp. 248–67 (orig. pub. 1900).

22 *Ibid.*, p. 258.

from primeval dream material, quoting Jocasta's speech that "many a man here now in dreams hath lain with her who bore him."

In *Totem and Taboo*,[23] published in 1913, Freud claimed an even wider universality for the oedipus complex and expressed a "suspicion" that it might underlie the primeval sense of guilt from which, in his view, religion and morality originally arose. Freud was an armchair anthropologist of the bad old school, pulling ethnographic facts out of context with cheerful unconcern, and *Totem and Taboo,* unlike his other serious works, is today embarrassingly dated.

His fullest description of the oedipus complex is contained in the *General Introduction to Psycho-Analysis.*[24] The emphasis is on the specifically neurotic character of the relationships between small boys and their mothers and between little girls and their fathers. (Freud never referred to an electra complex; the term was invented by his followers.) For Freud, the oedipus complex included the daughter's jealousy of her mother and rivalry between brothers and sisters as well as the replacement of parents as love objects by older siblings after a child is displaced by the arrival of other children. The theory is completed by an explanation of the incest taboo. The erotic objects chosen early in life are usually incestuous and the most stringent regulation is necessary to check men's sustained infantile desires for their mothers and sisters. In the psychoneurotic, these tendencies have been enlarged and elaborated, but —and this is a significant new element—we now learn that, in normal subjects as well, incestuous themes are taken up again in adolescence and incorporated into adult sexuality with renewed libidinal force. Thus, from puberty on, the "task" of the normal individual is emancipation from his parents. A son must abandon his desire for his mother and his hostility or subservience to his father, and a daughter must agree to forgive her mother and accept another man as lover in place of her father.

It is difficult to assess the implications of this theory for the theory of coalitions. Many ideas that seemed revolutionary or bizarre when Freud first propounded them have since been almost universally accepted. It is no longer shocking to hear that a child may hate a parent, repress the emotion, carry it forward into later life, and transfer it to another person. That infantile feelings affect later behavior, that small children have erotic inclinations, that love and hate may be felt simultaneously for the same person, that forbidden impulses may disappear from consciousness but continue to generate anxiety are now commonsense notions. Most of these notions have not been empirically demonstrated, but empirical

23 Sigmund Freud, *Totem and Taboo,* trans. James Strachey (London: Routledge & Kegan Paul, Ltd., 1950) (orig. pub. 1913).
24 Sigmund Freud, *General Introduction to Psycho-Analysis,* trans. Joan Riviere (New York: Garden City Publishing Co., 1943) (orig. pub. 1917).

demonstrations of the usual kind may not be feasible or necessary for the propositions of psychoanalytic theory.

The problem is with matters of fact. Freud's observation of Viennese family life together with his personal experience persuaded him that little boys love their mothers and little girls love their fathers with a sexual inclination that includes overt bodily attraction. His reading convinced him that this tendency was universal or nearly universal and in no way peculiar to his own milieu.

Yet, unless all factual references made in connection with psychoanalysis are to be given immunity from the rules of scholarly evidence, we must conclude that Freud was mistaken and that the coalitions of mother-son and father-daughter he observed represent no more than a local practice. Crosscultural studies show no universal learning toward this pattern. Indeed, it is rather rare. Mother-son coalitions are not uncommon under appropriate conditions, but they are seldom matched with symmetrical father-daughter coalitions. Mother-daughter coalitions occur frequently, although for different reasons, in both patriarchal and matriarchal families.

It may be argued, first, that coalitions, as we define them, are not the same as the libidinal attractions described by Freud, and second, that coalitions incompatible with the oedipal pattern may develop as defenses against forbidden oedipal passions.

Regarding the first point, we can only note that Freud describes the mutual attraction of mother and young son and of father and young daughter as reciprocated, deliberate, solidary, advantageous for both members in securing external goals, and directed against the other parent. If this is not a coalition, it is the same phenomenon under another name.

Regarding the second point, it is entirely reasonable to suppose that *any* coalition in the family is formed in order to prevent the formation of an alternative coalition, and that a parental coalition is a defensive move to forestall the parent-child coalition feared by a parent. It is also plausible that a parent-child coalition (especially between mother and son) that is conservative, supportive, and approved by the other parent when the child is young may seem threatening when the child becomes stronger and may then provoke a countercoalition.

The libidinal element remains. We cannot deny that the sentiments of small boys towards their mothers are qualitatively different than those aroused by their fathers, if only because male behavior is distinguishable from female behavior in all societies and because the initial relationship of mother and child is closer, more essential, and more crucial for the development of the child than the infant's relationship with his father. But it is not self-evident that the infant's physical attachment to his mother must develop into emotional solidarity with her as he matures, or that the sexual impulses of early childhood can distinguish accurately between social categories, or that little girls are less apt than little boys to look to their mother for sensual satisfactions, or that the father-daughter relationship is a mirror image of the mother-son relationship. The oedipus concept is a reminder that deep-rooted, unconscious libidinal motives play a large part in the selection of coalition partners and warns us against the attempt to explain family coalitions exclusively in terms of relative power, but the particular coalition pattern that Freud preferred and found wherever he looked for it appears to be only one of many possibilities.

GROWING UP WITH PARSONS AND BALES

The theory developed by Parsons and Bales and set forth in their notable volume on the family [25] is founded directly on Freudian thinking, but it manages to transform it into something quite different. The problem they set themselves to solve is how the nuclear family shapes a newborn infant without social habits into an adult member of a society ready to act as a parent himself. The other functions of the nuclear family are considered only as they impinge upon the process of socialization, and then only in general terms. The focus is on the urban middle-class American family, although both authors are sensitive to cultural variations.[26]

Because of their emphasis on socialization, Parsons and Bales are particularly interested in infancy and early childhood, especially the oedipal phase of child development which they describe engagingly as the child's movement "from integrated membership in a two-member (autonomous) interaction system where power and instrumental-expressive differentiation are fused, to integration in a four-member, or basic role, system, where these two axes of differentiation have become segregated out from each other." [27] What this means is that the child moves from exclusive involvement in a mother-child relationship to recognition of his father and siblings.

The basic proposition of the theory is that the structure of the nuclear family is a consequence of differentiation on two axes: that of hierarchy and power and that of instrumental and expressive functions. Thus, the family contains four *types* of status roles: instrumental superior, expressive superior, instrumental inferior, and expressive inferior. According

[25] Talcott Parsons and Robert F. Bales, *Family, Socialization and Interaction Process* (New York: Free Press of Glencoe, Inc., 1955).

[26] Their book includes a chapter by Morris Zelditch, Jr., reporting a crosscultural study of role differentiation in the nuclear family.

[27] Parsons and Bales, *op. cit.*, p. 77.

to these authors, differences of generation and sex symbolize the more fundamental differentiations of power and of instrumental-expressive functions. It is taken for granted that every parent is more powerful than every child (a reasonable assumption when discussing infancy) and that males specialize in instrumental, and females in expressive, functions. The instrumental function involves the family's adaptation to its environment and the achievement of external goals. The expressive function is the maintenance of close relationships among family members and the regulation of their emotions.

Parsons and Bales frequently ascribe the origin of their theory to the discovery that task-oriented, *ad hoc* groups in Bales' laboratory experiments showed certain similarities to the nuclear family. The laboratory groups tended to develop an "idea man" and a "best-liked man" who shared leadership. Parsons and Bales were struck by the similarity of this pattern to the differentiated roles of father and mother in the nuclear family.

Parsonian children differ from Freudian children in two important ways. First, they have fewer erotic feelings. The biological sex difference is a symbol for the social needs arising during socialization, not an independent drive.[28] Eroticism, from this point of view, is a reward for passing the course in socialization. The Parsonian child shows no precocious craving for carnal knowledge as he pursues the gratifications available at his stage of life.

The other important difference is the absence of any particular attraction between father and daughter. There is no trace of the electra complex in this model. Both boys and girls undergo an "oedipal crisis" involving the disruption of their initial exclusive attachments to the mother and the recognition of father and siblings. However, their situations are not identical. In order to participate in higher-order relationships, a girl must understand that she is different from her mother in one chief respect—generation—whereas a boy must adjust to being different in two chief respects—generation and sex—which is much more difficult, since acceptance of male identity requires that he shift from an expressive to an instrumental style of behavior. In the post-oedipal phase (which seems to begin at about age six) neither child has any special inclination towards the parent of the opposite sex.[29]

---

[28] "The pre-oedipal child is, we assume, in the sense of fundamental personality constitution, sexless—as is in literal terms the mother,·since we assume that *for the child* the differentiation of the two parents as objects by sex has not yet on the requisite level been internalized"—*ibid.*, p. 78.

[29] ". . . the role of the post-oedipal boy is *farthest* from that of the mother, she is the one family member with whom he shares *no* sub-collectivity identifications within the family, but only the overall familial identification. Correspondingly, the girl at this stage is farthest from the father role: she shares no sub-collectivities with him"—*ibid.*, p. 111.

The question of the relative power of husband and wife, which fascinates so many students of the family, hardly arises in this model. Power is something exercised by parents over children; almost all differences *between* parents are referred to the instrumental-expressive axis. The possibility that any winning coalition besides the parental coalition may occur in the primary triad seems to be ruled out. The nuclear family is described as an important structural component of all societies. Its cultural variability is limited, first, by the need to maintain a power differential in favor of the parents, and second, by the need to impose a husband-father role more instrumental and less expressive than the role of the wife-mother. Parsons and Bales' special interest in the earliest phases of socialization probably accounts for their insistence that the parental coalition is the only likely coalition in the nuclear family. In effect, their discussion of coalitions ends where ours began, at the point where the child may glimpse the possibility of entering a winning coalition with one of his parents.

We are left with the puzzle of why power differences between parents and between siblings are omitted from the Parsons and Bales model of the nuclear family. Does differentiation along an instrumental-expressive axis preclude differentiation of the same actors on a scale of influence or authority? Parsons and Bales make it clear that the two types of differentiation are not incompatible, since they describe instrumental fathers as exercising authority over expressive daughters, and expressive mothers as dominating instrumental sons. The omission may have been a mere oversight, but it is more likely that such differences were not taken into account because they appeared to be insignificant in comparison with the enormous difference of power between parents and helpless infants. Nothing in the model suggests that instrumental-expressive differentiation replaces or seriously modifies the power distribution that provides us with basic information about coalition possibilities. To the extent that coalitions are more readily formed between like than unlike partners, father-son and mother-daughter coalitions should be somewhat more frequent in families in which the instrumental-expressive differentiation is sharp. But this would be as true for any other qualitative characteristic.

The facts supporting this model are somewhat in dispute. The chapter by Zelditch, included in the original volume, provided impressive cross-cultural evidence for the existence of parental role differentiation nearly everywhere. But Slater,[30] a former collaborator of Parsons and Bales, has developed a devastating criticism of the claims that instrumental-expres-

---

[30] Philip Slater, "Parental Role Differentiation," *American Journal of Sociology,* XLVII, No. 3 (November 1961), 296–311.

sive role differentiation is universal in the nuclear family, that it facilitates the child's identification with the same-sex parent, and that it is essential to the normal development of the child. He drew on empirical studies of the modern American family to show that fathers are often more supportive and rewarding than mothers, that parental role differentiation seems to be *unfavorable* for the emotional adjustment of children, and that rigid differentiation along instrumental-expressive lines leads to alienation between fathers and sons.

THE HSU TYPOLOGY

An interesting contrast to these somewhat ethnocentric pictures of the nuclear family is provided by Hsu's sweeping typology of kinship and culture.[31] He identifies four major types of society in the world and proposes that each of them emphasizes a different relationship in the nuclear family and that many differences in language, social organization, religion and working habits can be traced back to this differentiation.

Societies of Type *A* emphasize the "father-son axis"; this group includes a majority of the peoples of the Orient, excluding India. Type *B* emphasizes the supremacy of the husband-wife relationship, and it includes most European societies and people of European origin throughout the world. Type *C* attaches primary importance to the mother-son axis; the Hindus are its typical representatives. Type *D* emphasizes the brother-brother axis; most African societies are said to fall into this category.

An emphasized relationship, as Hsu describes it, is not exactly a coalition but something quite similar. It is the "dominant axis" in a given kinship structure in two senses: first, it serves as a point of reference for all other relationships and determines their significance; and second, it provides the foundation of basic experience from which most of the values of individuals are derived. With the possible exception of Type *C,* it may be inferred from Hsu's discussion that coalitions along the dominant axis—the father-son coalition in China, the parental coalition in the United States, the fraternal coalition in Central Africa—will be systematically encouraged and approved of in their respective societies.

Type *A* societies emphasize the father-son relationship at the expense of all others; the characteristic content that arises from this emphasis is mutual dependence. Each individual is enmeshed in a network of continuous relationships extending far back into the past and indefinitely forward into the future. The son owes his father obedience, respect, and

31 Francis L. K. Hsu, "Kinship and Ways of Life: An Exploration," in *Psychological Anthropology: Approaches to Culture and Personality* (Homewood, Ill.: Richard D. Irwin, Inc., 1961).

support. The father owes the son protection and suitable provision. The network of kinsmen based on common patrilineal descent extends in all directions, and women are incorporated into their husbands' families and acquire patrilineal concerns. Romantic love is absent; its place is taken by filial duty. People living in this type of kinship pattern, says Hsu, will be conservative because their places in the web of kinship are fixed and there is little they can strive for independently. Since they grow up under the guidance of numerous adults, they learn to view the world in a relativistic way and to compromise easily.

Hsu goes much further:

> Our analysis here makes it clear that the Chinese lack an interest in abstraction because their anchorage in the web of human relations foredoomed the development of any scientific spirit and inquiry, in spite of an early history of science and invention.[32]

He explains oriental music and art in similar terms, as well as the tendency to centralized government that originates from submission to parental authority. Religion will be polytheistic, with a core of ancestor worship and with a multitude of beneficent personified gods. More than any other societies, those of Type *A* resist political and social change.

In the Type *B* society the basic unit in which children grow up is the nuclear family consisting of parents and unmarried children. Within the family all obligations are subordinated to the relationship of husband and wife, which is exclusive and discontinuous. Monogamy founded on romantic love is the ideal, and marriage is the only permanent bond, the parent-child relationship being virtually abrogated when the children become adults. The emphasis on the husband-wife relationship cuts each nuclear family adrift and gives it a life cycle of its own. Children grow up in the exclusive care and under the absolute control of their parents within a childhood world of drastically simplified moral values. Everything in this way of life imposes self-reliance on the individual. He is trained to think primarily of his own interests and to make his own place in the world. This emphasis encourages creativity on the one hand and conflict on the other. It facilitates innovation in language, art, and literature and instability in politics. The monolithic family pattern leads to monotheism, but at the same time individualism prevents religious unity and encourages the formation of sects. Lacking any permanence in their human relationships, men attach themselves to creeds, prejudices, and other abstractions, for which they fight bitterly; this is another impetus to social change.

Hindu society is the only example of Type *C* discussed by Hsu, although he supposes that the Moslems of India may fall into the same category. Hindu culture is acknowledged to be male-oriented, but the mother-son relationship is said to dominate the kinship pattern. The dependence of the son on the mother is maintained throughout childhood. Because the Hindu household is segregated by sex and children remain on the female side of the house, boys have little contact with their fathers and male relatives. The characteristic kinship content is described as supernatural dependence. The men in Type *C* cultures solve their problems either by passively abandoning their goals in the name of supernatural values or by taking part in elaborate rituals for the purpose of influencing the gods. The worshipper-dependent approaches his god in a demanding, emotional, childlike way, suffused with erotic symbolism. Religion and literature embody numerous contradictions because no necessity to develop a rational structure is felt. Political authority is secured either by exaggerated differentiation between superiors and inferiors or by a supernatural mystique. The disunity of beliefs and styles of life leads to internal dissatisfaction, but the pressure for change is diffuse. Cultural transformation is slow and generally superficial.

The majority of Africans south of the Sahara are said to live in Type *D* societies. Their kinship structures vary greatly, but they are said to emphasize the fraternal relationship, so that the ties between generations are overshadowed by those between males of the same generation. Type *D* societies show a good deal of mistrust and sorcery in the relationship between parents and children but not in that between brothers. Although ancestor worship is practiced in some African societies, the ancestral spirits are more likely to be threatening than benign. Age-grading customs have the double effect of separating parents from their children and of extending the fraternal bond to age-mates as well as to male cousins and other kin. The institution of blood brotherhood provides another means of fraternal extension. Competition for power is regarded as a contention of brothers. Type *D* societies are not strongly anchored to the past or strongly committed to the future, and although they may develop large-scale systems of trade, labor, and art, they do not develop stable governments. Their fraternal solidarity seems to be undermined by reactions similar to sibling rivalry.

Hsu himself insists that the evaluation of this thesis will require a great deal of empirical information about family structure that is not yet available. Thus, for the present his theory must be looked upon as speculative.

OTHER VIEWPOINTS

There is another school of thought that divides power in the family into several distinct components, either by assuming that each type of family activity has its own distribution of power, or that power in one relationship is independent of power in another, so that, for example, the husband who tyrannizes his wife may be weak and ineffective with his children. There is obvious merit in this approach, since common experience suggests that power distributions are never entirely consistent and that any interaction network is likely to be modified when actors change from one activity to another. Herbst [33] distinguishes four "regions" of family activity: household, children, social activity, and economic activity, and considers the possibility that either husband or wife may be dominant in any one of these "regions," although he or she may be dominated in another. In a study based on this scheme he found several patterns. In the *autonomic* pattern husband and wife are each dominant in at least one region and specialize in the activities they dominate. In the pattern of *husband dominance,* the essential decisions in each region are made by the husband, and the wife cooperates by carrying them out. This is reversed in the pattern of *wife dominance.* Finally in the *syncretic* pattern, decision-making and task performance are evenly shared.

Beginning with similar assumptions, Blood and Wolfe [34] questioned more than 900 married women in Detroit and surrounding areas. Each woman was asked who made the final decision with respect to eight choices made in the family: (1) what job the husband should take, (2) what car to buy, (3) whether to buy life insurance, (4) where to go on a vacation, (5) where to live, (6) whether the wife should work, (7) what doctor to go to, and (8) how much money to spend for food. The responses were rated numerically from 1 if the wife always decided a particular issue to 5 if the husband always decided it. Relative power was thus compared numerically from one issue to another.

For the sample as a whole, the findings were not surprising. Either these families were essentially egalitarian or the wives reported them to be so, or routine decisions of this kind do not reflect the essentials of dominance and submission. Husbands were reported to be responsible for decisions about jobs, cars, and insurance policies; wives for decisions about their own work, the family doctor, and the food budget. Vacation and residential decisions were reported as shared.

When the sample was broken down by respondent characteristics, the results were considerably more interesting. Contrary to expectation, Catholic and foreign-born husbands did not seem to be especially powerful at home. White husbands were significantly more dominant than

---

[33] P. G. Herbst, "Conceptual Framework for Studying the Family," in Oscar A. Oeser and S. B. Hammond, eds., *Social Structure and Personality in a City* (London: Routledge & Kegan Paul, Ltd., 1954), pp. 126–37.

[34] Robert O. Blood, Jr., and Donald L. Wolfe, *Husbands and Wives: The Dynamics of Married Living* (New York: Free Press of Glencoe, Inc., 1960).

Negroes, and white-collar workers more powerful than blue-collar workers. Husbands whose education exceeded their wives', who attended church more often than average, whose wives were not employed, and who were successful in their occupations had more influence over their wives. There is a striking correlation between the husband's decision-making power and his annual income. Most interesting, perhaps, is a table showing a longterm decline in the husband's power during the life cycle of the family. It seems to increase at the birth of the first child and then to decline steadily as the children become pre-adolescent, adolescent, and adult. At each age, however, the husband-father's power over his wife exceeds that of the husband in childless couples. The authors remark that

> Having a young child creates needs for the wife which lead her to depend more on her husband for help, for financial support and for making decisions. As children grow up, they shift from being burdens to being resources whom the wife draws upon in marital decision-making. They also become resources in other ways, providing companionship and emotional support which make the wife less dependent on her husband.
>
> However, the resources which growing children provide are meager in comparison to the extra-familial resources on which childless women can draw. Childlessness allows the continuation of the honeymoon state of mutual emotional and financial dependence with the husband. Moreover, the continued participation of the wife in the occupational world accelerates her own maturity toward decision-making resourcefulness.[35]

In general, these findings suggest that power and prestige earned in outside organizations can be imported into the family. The existence of alternative associates and activities would seem to strengthen the hand of a parent as much as the hand of a rebellious adolescent.

Another illustration of this principle is found in Elizabeth Bott's case study of the internal and external relationships of a small sample of nuclear families in England.[36] She discovered that both paternal authority and clearly differentiated conjugal roles were likely to be most pronounced in families having a closeknit network of external relationships with relatives and neighbors. Equalitarianism and a minimum division of labor were characteristic of isolated nuclear families enjoying little external support. The convergence is not as complete as may first appear because, in the families described by Bott, the wife has the closer ties with the external network, maintaining a particularly close relationship with her mother. The support this provides for the husband's authority can only be understood in the total context.

---

35 *Ibid.*, p. 42.
36 Elizabeth Bott, *Family and Social Network: Roles, Norms, and External Relationships in Ordinary Urban Families* (London: Tavistock Publications, 1957).

The distribution of power in a family may also be explored by examining each relationship as separate from and independent of other relationships. Bowerman and Elder [37] studied a large sample of families by administering questionnaires to the sons and daughters of these families in high school. Each family was classified according to *conjugal power structure*—the relationship between husband and wife, *parental role pattern*—the relative importance of each parent in relation to the responding adolescent, and *child rearing structure*—the degree of authority exercised by each parent separately. Not surprisingly, the achievements and aspirations of adolescents seem to be influenced much more by their own relations with each parent than by their parents' relationship with each other.

The work of Bowerman and Elder is part of a flourishing branch of family research that attempts to determine the influence of a family's power structure on the aspirations and achievements of its children. The original impetus comes from the work of David McClelland,[38] whose theory of modernization proposes that people are made fit or unfit to participate in a modernizing society by their childhood experiences. In general, McClelland and his followers expect that boys who are permitted to compete with their fathers in early life and who discover the possibility of rivaling him successfully are more apt to better themselves through the acquisition of industrial skills, to abandon local ties for distant opportunities, and to be generally more ambitious and adaptable than are those whose early experience teaches them the futility of defying Father and the local gods. In addition to considerable work in the United States,[39] comparative studies have been made in a number of other countries.[40]

[37] Charles E. Bowerman and Glen H. Elder, Jr., "Variations in Adolescent Perception of Family Power Structures," *American Sociological Review*, XXIX, No. 4 (August 1964), 551–67. For a study with a similar approach to family structure in a simple society, see Francesca Cancian, "Interaction Patterns in Zinacanteco Families," in the same issue of the *American Sociological Review*, pp. 540–50.

[38] David C. McClelland, *The Achieving Society* (Princeton, N.J.: D. Van Nostrand Co., Inc., 1961); David C. McClelland, *et al.*, *Talent and Society* (Princeton, N.J.: D. Van Nostrand Co., Inc., 1958); and David C. McClelland, John W. Atkinson, Russell Clark, and Edgar Lowell, *The Achievement Motive* (New York: Appleton-Century-Crofts, 1953).

[39] Admirably summarized by Uri Bronfenbrenner, in "Some Familial Antecedents of Responsibility and Leadership in Adolescence," in Luigi Petrullo and Bernard M. Bass, eds., *Leadership and Interpersonal Behavior* (New York: Holt, Rinehart & Winston, Inc., 1961), pp. 239–71.

[40] See, for example, Edward C. Devereaux, Uri Bronfenbrenner, and George J. Susi, "Patterns of Parents' Behavior in the United States of America and the Federal Republic of Germany: A Cross-National Comparison," *International Social Science Journal*, XIV (1962), 488–506; and Glen H. Elder, Jr., "Family Structure and Educational Attainment: A Cross-National Analysis," *American Sociological Review*, XXX, No. 1 (February 1965), 81–96.

All the studies agree in finding some relationship between family power structure and filial achievement in every sample examined up to the present time. When social class and community type are taken into account, the apparent effect of the family constitution on the behavior of its children may diminish sharply. The studies also seem to establish that nations, ethnic groups, social classes, and even localities have distinctive power configurations in the nuclear family, so that despite individual variation, it makes sense to speak of a typical American urban, Brazilian rural, or West German working-class family, describing any of these families by a characteristic power distribution.

The available evidence suggests that the role of the father is more crucial than that of the mother in determining behavioral outcomes for both sons and daughters. The reason for this is almost paradoxical, since under modern conditions the father's role in child raising is largely elective. In a given social setting the role of the mother may be seen as nearly a constant, all mothers behaving more or less alike. Differences in the behavior of children are often traceable to the father's role, which may vary from despotism to helplessness and from indifference to passionate devotion.

The findings seem to favor some measure of paternal dominance. There is evidence that maternal dominance induces greater conflict,[41] and there is also some indication that it contributes to schizophrenia and other grave troubles in children.[42] In this respect, even the equipotestal family can be criticized:

> But what if roles are undifferentiated so that both parents share equal responsibilities for discipline and control? Our data are not in the form best suited to answer this question. They do indicate, however, that the groups classified as Low in either responsibility or leadership tend to show the smallest absolute differences between parents' scores in discipline and power. In other words, the most dependent and least dependable adolescents describe family arrangements which are neither patriarchal nor matriarchal, but egalitarian. To state the issue in a more provocative form, our data suggests that the democratic family, which for so many years has been held up and aspired to as a model by professionals and enlightened laymen, tends to produce young people "who do not take the initiative," "look to others for direction and decision," and "cannot be counted on to fulfill obligations." [43]

41 Blood and Wolfe, *op. cit.*
42 See Melvin L. Kohn and John H. Clausen, "Parental Authority Behavior and Schizophrenia," *American Journal of Ortho-Psychiatry*, XXVI (April 1956), 297–313; and Theodore Lidz, Beula Parker, and Alice Cornelison, "The Role of the Father in the Family Environment of the Schizophrenic Patient," *American Journal of Psychiatry*, CXIII (1956), 126–32.
43 Bronfenbrenner, "Some Familial Antecedents . . . ," *op. cit.*, p. 267.

On the whole, the empirical data do not support the hypothesis that achievement in later life is the reward for escaping paternal domination. The adolescent is more likely to have problems in gaining emancipation from both parents, although these problems will not be identical. Both the benefits of emotional support and the dangers of oversupport must be considered in relation to both parents.

The studies have not yet led to simple formulas connecting family structure and filial achievement. Although they are plainly related, the relationship is not linear. Successful child raising seems everywhere to depend on avoiding extreme treatment, as defined by local norms, and on finding a golden mean between tyranny and neglect, possessiveness and alienation. When a universalistic value such as achievement motivation is looked for in systems that emphasize other values, the problem becomes much more complex since parents will be judged successful, at least by the investigator, only if they produce culturally deviant children. A further deterrent to oversimplification is that the effect of a given parental pattern may be quite different for boys and for girls. Bronfenbrenner summarizes research findings on the effects of child rearing in the American middle class as follows:

> . . . the major obstacle to the development of responsibility and leadership in boys stems from inadequate levels of parental support and authority. For girls, the principal danger lies in the possibility of oversocialization through an overdose of parental affection and control. . . . For boys, it is the absence of sufficient warmth or discipline which more frequently impairs dependability; for girls, it is an overdose of either variable that has deleterious effects.[44]

At the present time we do not know whether studies of socialization that take into account the child's inclusion or exclusion in coalitions and distinguish between the sympathetic authority of a coalition partner, the hostile authority of a coalition opponent, and the joint authority exercised by a parental coalition will help to untangle this unwieldy matrix of intimate relationships. Meanwhile it is useful to know that the happy family is likely to show moderate, rather than extreme, forms of the local customs, whatever they may be.

[44] *Ibid.,* pp. 268–69.

VII

OTHER
FAMILY TRIADS

A number of family triads besides those we have considered so far, occur in nearly every society and show certain constant features when crosscultural comparisons are made. Four of them will be discussed in this chapter, each interesting in its own right and in relation to our theory: grandparent-parent-child, the sibling triad, husband-wife-mother-in-law, and father-son-uncle.

GRANDPARENT-PARENT-CHILD

Warm, affectionate relationships between grandparents and grandchildren are normal in our own society and in many others, although the quality of such relationships is not at all uniform when they are examined in detail. For example, Nadel's important study of grandparenthood in the Sudan, to which we shall return shortly, describes mutual teasing, horseplay and indecent conversation as the conventional modes of interaction between grandparents and their grandchildren. A "joking relationship" of this kind cannot really be discerned in the contemporary American family even though mild teasing is permitted among us.

Many similar distinctions become blurred when relationships are tabulated for crosscultural analysis. Indeed, some degree of oversimplification is inevitable, if only because the relationships of grandfather-grandson, grandmother-grandson, grandfather-granddaughter, and grandmother-granddaughter, which necessarily differ, are not likely to be fully and separately reported for any society. Thus, one set of grandparents may be much closer than the other, either by the operation of a kinship rule or through the accidents of family history.

Serious interest in these relationships is quite recent; only two comparative studies are available, but their results are unusually clear. Both studies were stimulated by Radcliffe-Brown's suggestion that "friendly equality" develops between grandparent and grandchild to counterbalance the tension that the grandchild experiences in relation to his parents and the grandparent in relation to his own children because of parental authority.[1]

Nadel [2] compares ten Nuba tribes in the Sudan. In nine of the tribes the grandfather does not live with the nuclear family and is not involved in its management, and in all nine of these cases, grandfather and grandson have a joking relationship. The tenth tribe has a joint family system and the household is headed by the grandfather or a man of the grandfather's generation. In this case, there is a joking relationship between father and son but none between grandfather and grandson.

Nadel continued by considering two tribes of West Africa, the Nupe and Gbani, that seem to deviate from this pattern, combining a joking relationship between grandfather and grandson with a joint family headed by the grandfather. In these tribes the grandson is looked upon as the reincarnation of a deceased grandfather whose name he receives, and he is even expected to marry his widowed grandmother in nominal marriage. Nadel explains the joking relationship by proposing that this mystical belief leads a grandson and his living grandfather to treat each other as equals and to interact as equals.

Apple [3] selected seventy-five societies for which adequate information about grandparental relationships is available and tested two hypotheses. First, for societies in which relationships with grandchildren are the same with both sets of grandparents, she proposes that if the grandparental generation continues to exercise considerable authority over the parental generation after the children are born the relationship of

[1] A. R. Radcliffe-Brown, "On Joking Relationships," *Africa,* XIII (1940), 195–210; and "The Study of Kinship Systems," *Journal of the Royal Anthropological Institute,* LXXI (1941), 1–18. See also his *Structure and Function in Primitive Society* (London: Cohen & West, Ltd., 1952).

[2] S. F. Nadel, *The Foundations of Social Anthropology* (New York: Free Press of Glencoe, Inc., 1951), pp. 235–36.

[3] Dorrian Apple, "The Social Structure of Grandparenthood," *American Anthropologist,* LVIII (August 1956), 656–63.

the grandparents with the grandchildren will *not* be one of friendly equality. Conversely, if the grandparental generation has little or no authority over the parental generation after the children are born, the relationship *will* be one of friendly equality.

The results strongly support the hypothesis. Of thirty-six societies in which grandparents have little or no authority over parents, thirty-two show friendly equality between grandparent and grandchild. Of fifteen societies in which grandparents exercise considerable authority over parents, only three show friendly equality between grandparent and grandchild.

For societies in which the relationship with one set of grandparents is formally differentiated from that with the other, the hypothesis is that if the grandchildren's relationship with one set of grandparents is marked by "less friendly equality," the less friendly grandparents will be found on the side of the parent or lineage exercising more authority in the nuclear family.

The correlation evoked by this hypothesis is almost perfect. Of seventeen societies with a preponderance of household authority on the father's side, all seventeen show less friendly equality with paternal grandparents. Of seven societies with the preponderance of household authority on the mother's side, six show less friendly equality with maternal grandparents.

For a subsample of societies, the investigator can demonstrate that these relationships are unaffected by the amount or severity of parental authority over children.

Apple's hypotheses can easily be converted into triadic form. Her first hypothesis, so far as can be determined,[4] refers to triads that are predominantly of Type 6: $A > B > C$, $A > (B + C)$, with either a parent or a grandparent as A. A dominates B and C, whether separately or in combination. No revolutionary coalition is possible, and A has no motive to form a superfluous coalition with either B or C. However, the conservative coalition BC is advantageous for both partners. When A is the intervening parent, this coalition has the interesting feature that the declining powers of grandparent B are balanced over time by the increasing strength of child C. The conservative character of the coalition enables the grandfather to participate in it without compromising his role as transmitter of traditional values and supporter of the status quo. In our own society, for example, this coalition basks in unqualified social approval. The grandchild, of course, benefits from the coalition outside as well as inside

---

4 Some of the societies included in Apple's sample are not fully described; for more than a third of them information about one or more grandparental or grandfilial positions is lacking.

the triad, since the alliance carries over into other situations in which he may benefit from the grandparent's status in the larger community.

Apple's second finding, that friendly equality with grandparents is more likely to develop on the side of the less authoritative parent or lineage, implies different power distributions in the triads paternal grandparent-father-child and maternal grandparent-mother-child, but the data are too sparse for further analysis. Although we know the names of the twenty-four societies included in the test of Apple's second hypothesis, we cannot even begin to describe their power distributions in such fine detail.

There is another way of translating the correlation discovered by Apple into triadic terms, although it is not entirely satisfactory. In place of three-generation triads, we might examine the triad paternal grandparent-maternal grandparent-grandchild, a triad which contains all the elements necessary for understanding the correlation. Unfortunately, we cannot be sure that there is an active relationship between paternal and maternal grandparents. In modernized urban communities the grandparents of a child are sometimes so distant, geographically or socially, that no perceptible relationship develops between them, and in the little societies studied by the anthropologists, exogamous arrangements may sometimes produce a similar effect. Nevertheless, under certain conditions the triad composed of a grandchild and his opposite grandparents will be important and active. It will be a triad of either Type 5 or Type 7, with the stronger grandparent as A, the other grandparent as B, and the child as C. If the difference in authority between the two lineages is barely appreciable, A and B should not differ much in power, and the coalition BC will be revolutionary and winning. If grandparent A is overwhelmingly dominant, the BC coalition will be conservative and nonwinning but clearly advantageous to both partners.

SIBLING TRIADS

Hardly any aspect of family life has been studied less than the interaction of siblings. We know that in our own society coalitions often develop in sibling triads during childhood and persist into adult life. In some preliterate societies, coalitions of brothers against an older sister or of any pair of younger siblings against an older are frequent and even formalized. But in the absence of systematically collected evidence, we are necessarily limited to some general issues.

We start by asking whether sibling rivalry is a normal pattern of behavior in a given type of nuclear family and, if so, between which siblings does it occur. A triad of siblings is usually linked (or has been linked in the past) to triads that include their parents. Hence, a sibling coalition is often the outcome of the coalition process in a superior triad involving a parent. When the parental coalition is so solidary that no child is ever allowed to form a winning coalition with one parent against the other, we may expect to see strong coalitions among the children and even a condition of general solidarity uniting all the children of a large family. When one parent is clearly dominant, a conservative coalition is likely to form between the weaker parent and a child, which may lead in turn to the formation of sibling coalitions against the favorite child or to other very complicated patterns in a sizable family. When father and mother are nearly equal in power but do not have a strong parental coalition, sibling rivalry will be intense and bitter as the children compete among themselves for the shifting coalition opportunities offered by their parents.

The lone empirical investigation that has been made in this area is hardly more than a pilot study, but its results are extremely interesting.[5] Fifty sibling triads in the families of Minnesota students were described by retrospective interviews with all of the 150 persons involved. Each triad was described as of the year the youngest sibling reached his tenth birthday. Of the fifty triads, twenty-three contained coalitions, counting only those coalitions verified by the separate reports of all three siblings. Fifteen were AB coalitions, seven were BC coalitions, and only one was an AC coalition. (The members of each triad were designated A, B, and C in order of age, anticipating that power would generally follow the same order.) Three of the BC coalitions were composed of twins, being all the twins in the sample. All but two of the twenty-three coalitions involved siblings of the same sex, and the average age difference between coalition partners was considerably less than that between the opponents and the nearest partner. These coalitions typically persisted into adulthood, with a tendency for the partners to continue their close associations after leaving the parental home.

The AB coalition clearly occurred the most frequently. This is not what we would anticipate either in the hierarchical Type 5 triad, in which the revolutionary coalition BC would be expected to occur, or in the Type 7 triad, in which the conservative coalition BC would offer so many advantages. But the findings make very good sense if we visualize these sibling triads as belonging to Type 1, or *peer* triads. In the middle-class, Midwestern families from which the sample was drawn, older siblings have no substantial power. They lack any vestige of jural authority and

5 Joel Gerstl, *Coalitions in the Sibling Triad* (Minneapolis: University of Minnesota, Department of Sociology, 1956) (mimeographed). For more general information, see Donald P. Irish, "Sibling Interaction: A Neglected Aspect in Family Life Research," in Bernard Farber, ed., *Kinship and Family Organization* (New York: John Wiley & Sons, Inc., 1966), p. 149–58.

are not permitted to reward or punish younger brothers and sisters in any way that might attract the attention of their parents. Furthermore, brothers are not entitled to dominate sisters. We cannot be certain that these conditions prevailed in all or most of the families in the sample, but the assumption that they did is not implausible, and it leads to a tentative interpretation of the findings.

The members of a peer triad need not be absolutely identical in power. Indeed, it is almost impossible to imagine complete equality persisting for more than a very brief time. The equality that defines a Type 1 triad is present if no member of the triad can depend on dominating another member in the presence of the third.

In theory, and in laboratory games, coalitions in Type 1 triads are highly unstable, because the opponent is always in a good position to entice one of the partners out of the coalition. Even in the laboratory this instability is disturbing, and experimental subjects try to stabilize their coalitions on some basis other than the power distribution. In Vinacke and Arkoff's original test of my hypotheses,[6] the ninety pachisi games with a Type 1 distribution produced thirty-three AB, thirty BC, and only seventeen AC coalitions. The investigators were puzzled by the surplus of BC over AC coalitions. Apparently, the subjects seized upon proximity in lettering or seating as a basis for the selection of partners in the absence of more relevant criteria.[7]

In the Minnesota study twenty-one of twenty-three sibling coalitions involved partners of the same sex, and for the sample as a whole, the age difference between coalition partners was considerably less than between nonpartners. Partners seem to have been chosen because of similarity first of sex, then of age. If we expand these few cases into a general model, coalitions would be expected in mixed-sex sibling triads in which the two siblings alike in sex were also adjacent in age. When the like-sex siblings were not adjacent in age, fewer coalitions would be formed. If all siblings were of the same sex, either AB or BC coalitions might form, with a possible preponderance of AB coalitions arising from the peculiarity that B, the middle brother, is more likely to perceive himself as similar to his older brother A than to his younger brother C when the differences in age are approximately the same.

In sum, because coalition partners in peer triads often select each other on the basis of likeness,[8] power distributions alone cannot explain

6 See pp. 24–25 above.

7 W. Edgar Vinacke and Abe Arkoff, "An Experimental Study of Coalitions in the Triad," *American Sociological Review*, XXII, No. 4 (August 1957), Table 1, p. 409.

8 Rosenthal discovered a parallel pattern of choosing coalition partners on the basis of likeness in a study of political coalitions in France. See Howard Rosenthal, *Simulating Elections in Western Democracies* (Pittsburgh: Carnegie Institute of Technology, 1967) (mimeographed).

coalition formation in triads in which differences of power are insignificant.

COLD AND WARM RELATIONSHIPS

Among the societies for which Apple found a nearly perfect correlation between authority on one side of the family and friendly equality with the grandparents on the other side, there are some societies in which a grandparent on the authoritative side exercises no direct authority over the child; but his relationship with the person who does exercise this authority prevents an easy, warm friendship with a grandchild. In a great many societies two categories of relationships with close relatives can be recognized: they may be called "cold" and "warm." The cold relationships are associated with severe authority, competing material interests, differences in class or clan affiliation, and so forth. The warm relationships are not hampered by formal authority, competing interests, strict taboos, or conflicting loyalties.[9] A triad that contains a warm relationship and two cold relationships is almost certain to develop a coalition. Indeed, the tendency to form a coalition whenever possible might be taken as an operational definition of the warm relationship.

The results of Apple's study plus a great deal of similar evidence demonstrate that warm and cold relationships generated in the nuclear family are readily extended along the lines of classificatory kinship, or, more precisely, that they are transitive, so that (1) the warm relatives of my warm relatives are warm to me, (2) the cold relatives of my warm relatives are cold to me, (3) the warm relatives of my cold relatives are cold to me, and (4) if we interact at all, the cold relatives of my cold relatives may be warm to me. In extended families in which little authority is exerted outside the nuclear family, the warmth of relationships may be far more important than differences of power in accounting for the coalitions observed.

[9] The necessary vocabulary for describing warm and cold relationships is often provided by the local culture as part of its kinship terminology. For example: "The Tikopia distinguish two categories of kinsfolk of the highest importance in the regulation of the social life. These are *tautau laui* and *tautau tariki,* in literal terms, the categories of good relationship and bad relationship, but implying here not a moral judgment as to the character of the relationships themselves but a distinction between the type of behavior permissible in conducting them. Freedom in the first case, restraint in the second, are the watchwords. To the first category belong the relationships of brothers, of mother's brother and sister's child, and to some extent, of grandparent and grandchild. Details of these have already been given. To the second category belong the relationships of parent and child, especially father and son, father's sister and her brother's children, and above all, affinal relatives"—Raymond Firth, *We the Tikopia: A Sociological Study of Kinship in Primitive Polynesia* (Boston: Beacon Press, 1963), p. 261 (orig. pub. 1936).

TABLE 7-1

Patterned Behavior Between a Man and His Female Relatives in Murdock's Sample of 250 Societies [10]

Relative	Avoidance or Marked Restraint	Respect or Reserve	Informality or Intimacy	Joking or Familiarity	Extreme Joking or License	Total Reporting
			Prescribed Behavioral Style			
Mother-in-law	78	33	26	0	0	129
Daughter-in-law	35	29	22	2	0	88
Sister	30	29	17	3	0	79
Mother's sister's daughter	17	24	9	3	0	53
Younger brother's wife	18	16	16	13	8	71
Father's brother's daughter	15	24	11	4	0	54
Father's sister's daughter	13	17	7	15	2	54
Mother's brother's daughter	11	19	9	13	1	53
Wife's elder sister	14	17	16	16	9	72
Father's sister	6	30	5	9	0	50
Wife's younger sister	8	14	19	20	9	70
Daughter	2	28	11	0	0	41
Mother	0	22	20	0	0	42
Mother's mother	0	16	14	14	0	44
Father's mother	0	16	13	15	0	44

[10] Adapted from Table 79 in *ibid.*, p. 277.

MOTHER-IN-LAW AVOIDANCE

The model example of a cold relationship is that between mother-in-law and son-in-law. In an astonishing number of societies, including our own, it is the most nervous and uncomfortable relationship in the entire network of kinship.

> In more than three-fifths of the world's societies, severe penalties follow upon the meeting of a man and his mother-in-law, and they shun each other accordingly. In northern Australia a man who speaks to his mother-in-law must be put to death. In parts of the South Pacific, both parties would commit suicide. In Yucatan, men believe that to meet one's mother-in-law face to face would render a man sterile for life, so he may travel miles out of his way over dangerous territory to avoid being near her. Navaho men believe that they will go blind if they see their mothers-in-law, so that she is not even allowed to attend the wedding.[11]

Murdock [12] tabulated patterned and prescribed behavior between the adult male and his female relatives, as reported for 250 societies by considerably more than 250 observers (see Table 7–1). The available information was fragmentary; each relationship—with one exception—was more frequently ignored than noted in the observers' reports. The exception was the relationship of a man to his wife's mother, which was recorded for 137 societies. The next most salient relationship, that of a man with his daughter-in-law, was recorded for only 88 societies.

Each relationship was classified under one of five headings: (1) avoidance or marked restraint, (2) respect or reserve, (3) informality or intimacy, (4) joking or familiarity, and (5) license or extreme joking. The first two categories are obviously "cold"; the next three are "warm."

A man's relationship with his wife's mother is likely to be rather chilly. In 57 per cent of the societies for which evidence is available he will avoid her or treat her with marked restraint, and in an additional 24 per cent, with respect or reserve. In the entire extensive sample there is no instance of joking, familiarity, or license as the *prescribed* form of behavior with a mother-in-law.

Murdock accepts the common belief that "mother-in-law taboos have the function of preventing sexual intercourse under circumstances peculiarly disruptive of interfamily cooperation." [13] He goes on to explain that for a man to have sexual intercourse with his mother-in-law would

---

11 John M. Shlien, "Mother-in-Law: A Problem in Kinship Terminology," in Hyman Rodman, ed., *Marriage, Family and Society* (New York: Random House, Inc., 1965), pp. 198–99.
12 George Peter Murdock, *Social Structure* (New York: The Macmillan Company, 1949).
13 *Ibid.*, p. 279.

create in his wife's nuclear family the kind of sexual rivalry that is prevented among the original members of the nuclear family by incest
taboos. The theory that mother-in-law avoidance is a simple device for
sexual regulation gains some support from the fact that avoidance between father-in-law and daughter-in-law is also widespread, appearing
in 40 per cent of the tabulatable cases in Murdock's sample.

The principal objection to this view is that in many societies, including
our own, the relationship between daughter-in-law and mother-in-law is
equally tense, and something like avoidance is commonly practiced
between the two women without any implication of sexual rivalry (except in the Freudian sense, which is not relevant to this argument). Similarly, in many societies a man avoids his father-in-law as much as or
more than he avoids his mother-in-law, and he expresses similar sentiments
towards both, although the possibility of sexual rivalry cannot have the
same influence on the relationship between him and his father-in-law.

Another objection to the view of mother-in-law avoidance as a form
of incest taboo is that no society in Murdock's sample (or outside it,
as far as I know) requires avoidance between a man and his own mother,
as might be expected if avoidance were primarily a device for preventing
disruptive sexual relationships within the nuclear family.

Although mother-in-law avoidance has overtones of hostility in many
societies, including our own this feature is not universal. Radcliffe-Brown
points out that

> This avoidance must not be mistaken for a sign of hostility. One does, of
> course, if one is wise, avoid having too much to do with one's enemies, but
> that is quite a different matter. I once asked an Australian native why he had
> to avoid his mother-in-law, and his reply was, "Because she is my best friend
> in the world; she has given me my wife." The mutual respect between son-
> in-law and parents-in-law is a mode of friendship. It prevents conflict that
> might arise through divergence of interest.[14]

There is an intellectual pitfall in the notion of universal mother-in-law
avoidance. Murdock's table shows informality or intimacy between a man
and his wife's mother in 19 per cent of the societies tabulated, and the
relationship is probably quite comfortable in some of the 113 societies
in the same sample in which no one noticed how a man treats his
mother-in-law. Although Americans may joke about their mothers-in-law
and do not seem to have a fixed term of address for them,[15] it is hard
to believe that any of the sacred horror that surrounds an encounter with
a mother-in-law in the Australian bush is felt in our system or that the

[14] A. R. Radcliffe-Brown, *Structure and Function in Primitive Society* (London:
Cohen & West, Ltd., 1952), p. 92.
[15] See Shlien, *op. cit.,* pp. 198–99.

aversion against incest is aroused by the report that a man has slept with his mother-in-law.

Even marriage to a mother-in-law is not universally prohibited. Mead [16] reports such marriages among the Mundugumor when, for example, a man marries a widow with a daughter and later marries the daughter, although powerful hostility develops between mother and daughter in consequence. It is easy to merge very different situations into a cross-cultural category like "avoidance." [17]

Nevertheless, there do appear to be some nearly universal features of living with or avoiding a mother-in-law. First, the patterned relationship is generally "cold" even in societies like our own that do not forbid the occasional development of a warm relationship. Second, whatever constraints are observed in relation to mothers-in-law are part of a set of constraints involving other affinal kin. Where a man avoids his mother-in-law, he may also avoid his father-in-law, treat his brother-in-law with gingerly politeness, and approach his brother-in-law's wife with prudish formality.

The basic assumption of triad theory is that the relationship between any pair of actors can best be understood by examining their conjoint relationships with significant third parties. In the nuclear family all members are significant third parties for any other pair. But in relationships between affinal relatives, the connecting spouse is likely to be *the* significant third party. Thus, we may hope to understand the relationship between a man and his wife's mother by examining the relationship of each to the woman between them.

The point of "mother-in-law avoidance" is that it *prevents* the otherwise inevitable formation of the triad—*husband-wife-wife's mother*. Avoidance may even be regarded as a social device for maintaining linked relationships among three actors without allowing them to form a triad. The triads suppressed in this way (either by a social norm or by individual choice) are thought of as unworkable. There can be many reasons for the unworkability of a triad, for example, the absence of a common language between A and C when A and B communicate in one language and B and C in another, or some physical barrier between one pair of actors. But these cases are trivial. The unworkable triads that matter are those that contain two incompatible coalitions and cannot resolve the problem either by the abandonment of one coalition or the development of triadic solidarity.

16 Margaret Mead, *Sex and Temperament in Three Primitive Societies* (New York: William Morrow & Co., Inc., 1935), pp. 208–9.

17 For a good account of the variation that may develop within a single society, see Vera St. Ehrlich, *Family in Transition: A Study of 300 Yugoslav Villages* (Princeton, N.J.: Princeton University Press, 1966).

The coalition of husband and wife is the most common of all family coalitions and is expected to occur as a matter of course in most societies. Mother and daughter coalitions are almost equally widespread and may arise from many different configurations of the nuclear family; they may evolve as conservative coalitions under strong paternal authority, revolutionary coalitions against weak paternal authority, authoritative coalitions in matripotestal systems, or even as peer coalitions in extremely egalitarian families. Most of the possible forms of the nuclear family seem to encourage coalitions between mothers and their adult daughters. Recent research has discovered, with some surprise, the strength of this bond in modern urban families.[18]

In the typical case, the activation of the triad *husband-wife-wife's mother* would confront the wife with an intolerable choice between two valuable coalitions, one indispensable in her family of origin, and the other in the family she has entered. This choice would first present itself in the early stages of marriage when the wife would be the inferior member of both coalitions, subordinate to her mother as well as to her husband, and fearful of offending either one. It may be juridically as well as psychologically difficult for her to choose between these conflicting authorities when both have legitimate rights over her.

A triad cannot function when it contains two coalitions. If neither coalition can be given up, the alternative to dissolving one of the coalitions is triadic solidarity. But this requires all three relationships to be "warm," a condition extremely difficult to satisfy in the triad of husband-wife-wife's mother. The mere fact of membership in different but linked nuclear families implies more difference of interest than a warm relationship permits. In addition to the hint of inadmissable sexual rivalries, a coalition between a man and his mother-in-law becomes unthinkable as soon as we identify it, as we must in linked triads, as a coalition *against* the father-in-law, the wife's brother, the husband's mother, and sundry other persons in the kinship network.

The above is all relevant to patterned, prescribed, stylized behavior and explains why there are few societies in which friendly solidarity between a man and his mother-in-law is the norm, although the conditions for such solidarity may exist in individual cases. In our own family system a troublesome wife who has been a difficult daughter may sometimes drive her husband and mother into a rueful coalition. Even the solidary triad is sometimes seen when the mother-in-law lives with her

18 W. J. H. Sprott, *Human Groups* (Baltimore: Penguin Books, Inc., 1958), pp. 61–64. See also Elizabeth Bott, *Family and Social Network* (London: Tavistock Publications, 1957); and Marvin B. Sussman and Lee G. Burchinal, "Kin Family Network: Unheralded Structure in Current Conceptualizations of Family Functioning," in Farber, ed., *op. cit.*, pp. 123–33.

married daughter or nearby and has no commitment to other close relatives. Isolated instances of joking relationships may even be observed, although no society seems to *prescribe* a joking relationship between a man and his wife's mother.

JOKING RELATIONSHIPS

Murdock's tabulation of prescribed behavior towards a man's female relatives contains a number of puzzles and inconsistencies that probably cannot be resolved without more comprehensive information than is now available. Most of the lines in the table are based on information obtained from only a fraction of the societies in the sample; ethnographic reports do not usually include a complete inventory of family relationships.

Despite these limitations, the table tells us a great deal about joking relationships. Stylized joking is never prescribed with one's own wife or mother. A man never avoids his grandmothers but very often jokes with them. Both joking and avoidance are frequent (in different societies, of course) in relation to cross-cousins—mother's brother's daughter and father's sister's daughter—but there is much more avoidance than joking when parallel cousins are involved. A man's female relatives of his own generation with whom he is expected to joke (usually his brothers' wives, his wife's sisters, or his cross-cousins) are those whom he might have married, or may still marry, or may seduce without opprobrium.

Neither of the two prevailing explanations fits these facts perfectly. Radcliffe-Brown's theory [19] that joking and avoidance are alternative ways of conducting a relationship in which there is both conjunction and divergence of interests does not begin to explain why the relationship with a given relative in a given society is characterized by joking or avoidance, but not by a choice of either, or why mothers-in-law are never joked with and grandmothers never avoided. Brant's theory [20] that joking foreshadows a sexual relationship does not help us understand why grandmothers and uncles are so often teased despite ingenious efforts to explain that in some tribes men marry their classificatory grandmothers or that one jokes with an uncle because one is expected to pursue his daughter if he has one. Neither theory really explains why men are more likely to avoid their parallel cousins on both sides than their cross-cousins.

A clue to the meaning of the joking relationship is that it is never

[19] Radcliffe-Brown, "On Joking Relationships," *op. cit.*, and "A Further Note on Joking Relationships," in *Structure and Function in Primitive Society, op. cit.*, pp. 90–116.

[20] C. S. Brant, "On Joking Relationships," *American Anthropologist*, L, No. 1 (January 1948), 160–62.

prescribed between husband and wife no matter how touchy their senti-ments may be. Joking seems to deny a coalition in circumstances in which a coalition might be expected to develop. The denial is public and ex-plicit, but it is mingled with friendliness towards the nonpartner—in sum, the relationship is warm. The refusal to form a coalition is signaled by insults, teasing, and disrespectful gestures. In a joking relationship between relatives the obligations of kinship are either abrogated—the boy need not obey his uncle—or parodied—he interprets his grandmother's affection as amorous passion. The joking pair behave frivolously towards each other to assure their potential opponent—and perhaps themselves—that they have not formed a real coalition against him.

If this interpretation is correct we would expect to find stylized joking relationships in triads in which there is an obvious opportunity for a disruptive coalition. The threatened coalition would be either revolu-tionary or improper. The joking and horse-play announce to the threat-ened third party that no coalition has been formed between the other two and that their friendship or their love affair need not be taken seriously by others towards whom they have more serious obligations. As Murdock's table illustrates, joking relationships are most likely to occur with three sorts of female relatives—grandmothers, sisters-in-law, and cross-cousins. In the first two categories, the identity of the potential opponent is self-evident. By joking with his grandmother a man shows that no conspiracy has been hatched from their mutual affection against the intervening parent, and by joking with his sister-in-law, particularly in tribes where he is allowed to make love to her, a man demonstrates that his allegiance to his wife remains unchanged.

In the case of cross-cousins the possibilities are more intricate. The potential opponent is a parent of one of the joking pair and the aunt or uncle of the other. To understand the triads formed when a man interacts with his cross-cousin, especially his mother's brother's daughter in a patrilineal system, we must consider an entire matrix of relationships involving the mother's brother.

THE KIND UNCLE AND FAVORITE NEPHEW

The role of the mother's brother in the patrilineal family has been a major theme of kinship studies since the appearance in 1924 of Rad-cliffe-Brown's short paper, "The Mother's Brother in South Africa." [21] In a study of the Ba Thonga people of Portuguese Africa some years be-fore Junod [22] had noted the peculiar relationship of mother's brother

21 Radcliffe-Brown, *Structure and Function in Primitive Society, op. cit.,* Chap. I.
22 Henri Junod, *The Life of a South African Tribe* (New Hyde Park, N.Y.: Univer-sity Books, 1962), 2 vols. (orig. pub. 1912).

and sister's son and concluded that it represented a vestige of an ancient matriarchal stage. Radcliffe-Brown set out to refute this view by showing that affection between the mother's brother and the sister's son or "uterine nephew" is a functional consequence of patriarchal authority.

Among the Ba Thonga the nephew enjoys the special solicitude of his uncle throughout his life. When he is sick, the uncle offers sacrifices on his behalf. He is permitted to take many liberties with his uncle, has some claim on his uncle's estate, and is entitled to steal food and drink from his uncle. Very similar customs had been recorded elsewhere, especially among the Nama Hottentots, and among the Tonga of Polynesia, half a world away from the Ba Thonga. The Ba Thonga as well as the Tonga have a term for mother's brother that translates approximately as *male mother*. In some of these same tribes, the father's sister is treated with particular respect and obedience.

The attitudes developed towards maternal uncles and paternal aunts are extended, with reduced intensity, towards remoter relatives in the same classification, such as cross-cousins. The same attitudes may even be extended to their household gods and expressed in rituals like the stealing of sacrifices.

Radcliffe-Brown attributes this entire complex of behavior to an original differentiation of attitudes within the nuclear family whereby the obligations of obedience and respect developed towards the father are generalized and extended towards all paternal kin and the expectations of care and indulgence from the mother became attached to her kin in varying degrees according to the closeness of relationship.

This simple, straightforward idea has been greatly elaborated by later theorists drawing on evidence from about a dozen other societies with somewhat similar patterns. The significance of the pattern is underscored by the matrilineal Trobrianders,[23] among whom a boy's maternal uncle commands obedience and respect and his own father treats him something like a favorite nephew, the Kgatla, who pair siblings in such a way that "a man's linked sister is also the linked paternal aunt of his children, just as he is the linked maternal uncle of hers," [24] and the Tikopia,[25] who call the uterine nephew *tama tapu*, "sacred child," and express the solicitude of maternal uncles in elaborate ceremonies.

Radcliffe-Brown continued by suggesting that in strongly patriarchal societies, such as those of the Ba Thonga and the Tonga, "the father is the one who must be respected and obeyed, and the mother is the one

---

23 See the various reports of Bronislaw Malinowski, esp. *The Father in Primitive Psychology* (New York: W. W. Norton & Company, Inc., 1927).

24 I. Schapera, *Married Life in an African Tribe* (Evanston: Northwestern University Press, 1966), p. 110.

25 Firth, *op. cit.*, pp. 198 ff.

from whom may be expected tenderness and indulgence," [26] and that the same kind of behavior tends to be extended to all the maternal relatives, including, of course, the mother's brother. He then proceeded to state that in a strongly matriarchal society the mother's brother might be the person to be respected and obeyed, since he has powers of life and death over his nephew. He did not maintain, as some of his followers imagine, that the father's sister in a matriarchal system is treated like the mother's brother in a patriarchal system, if only because he had no relevant data. So far as I know, to this day, no one has yet described a matrilineal system in which the relationship between a man and his father's sister mirrors the characteristic attachment to a mother's brother in a patrilineal system.

Nor has anyone shown that maternal uncles in our own society are more likely than paternal uncles to favor a nephew in families in which the father is authoritarian and the mother indulgent. The favorite nephew relationship does not play an important part in Western literature or mythology. Although it is associated with patriarchalism, it is not to be found in every patriarchal society.

THE "NATURAL TRIAD"

Freilich identifies the system composed of son, father, and mother's brother in patrilineal societies as the "natural triad," in which "the biological terms *father, mother's brother, son* and *sister's son* may usefully be replaced by structural-functional terms emphasizing positions and activities. The basic elements of the system discussed are the status roles: *High-Status Authority, High-Status Friend* and *Low-Status Subordinate.*" [27]

Freilich refers to these three positions as *HSA, HSF,* and *LSS,* and suggests that in a matrilineal society, the mother's brother will become the *HSA* while the father becomes the *HSF.* Similarly, he points out that maternal grandparents can play the role of *HSF* when authority lies on the father's side of the family, and a paternal grandparent may be the *HSF* in families dominated by maternal kin. He does not discuss the instances in which both sets of grandparents have authority nor those in which neither set has authority.

Other examples of "natural triads" that Freilich mentions are warden-chaplain-prisoner, hospital psychiatrist-social worker-patient, army officer-chaplain-G. I., and authoritarian professor-friendly professor-student. The conditions shared by these groups are the following:

26 *Ibid.,* p. 20.
27 Morris Freilich, "The Natural Triad in Kinship and Complex Systems," *American Sociological Review,* XXIX, No. 4 (August 1964), 530.

First, *three status-roles* are present in a subsystem containing at least two status positions. Second, one status-role *(LSS)* has lower status than the other two status-roles *(HSA* and *HSF* respectively). Third, *LSS* is a common alter to both *HSA* and *HSF.* Fourth, the dyadic relationship *HSA-LSS* is that between a superordinate and a subordinate such that (a) the position of *HSA* is that of a jural or legitimate authority, based on "rational," "traditional," or "charismatic" grounds, or on a combination of these; (b) *HSA* initiates activities for *LSS* and not vice versa; and (c) the dominant type of sentiment in the relationship *HSA-LSS* could be described as *negative,* ranging from formality and considerable restraint to dislike and hate. Fifth, in the relationship *HSF-LSS,* status differences are "played down," so that (a) the relationship can be described as based on "friendly equality" and intimacy; (b) the intimate content of the relationship tends to be initiated by the *LSS; LSS* confides in, "takes liberties with," cries on the shoulder of *HSF* and not vice versa; and (c) the dominant type of sentiment in the relationship could be described as *positive,* ranging from strong regard and admiration to liking and loving.[28]

Freilich suggests several explanations for the supposed ubiquity of this pattern. He sees the coalition of *HSF* and *LSS* as a socially useful check on the power of *HSA* and also as a means of reducing the tension created by the exercise of authority in the system as a whole and within the psyches of the immediate participants. A father who develops tension by exercising paternal authority can reduce it by moving into another subsystem in which he plays the role of mother's brother to his sister's son. Freilich, drawing on the work of Bales in small experimental groups, identifies the *HSA* of a natural triad as its "task specialist" and *HSF* as its "social-emotional specialist," assuming that both these leadership roles must be enacted in every group, preferably by different persons. He suggests that problems arise in the American nuclear family when one parent attempts to enact both roles.

He then considers the natural triad in terms of Heider's balance theory. Theoretically, interaction will be balanced if all three relationships are positive or if two relationships are negative. The latter he envisages as the normal condition, with *HSF* and *LSS* united by positive sentiments (liking, helping, admiring, etc.) and both of them separated from *HSA* by negative sentiments (hating, injuring, admonishing, etc.). A negative relationship between *HSA* and *HSF* is essential to the constitution of the natural triad as it is described.

Freilich does not actually show that the relationships between *HSA* and *HSF* are negative in the examples he uses. Indeed, it may not be possible to do so. The Tikopian family is the central case in Freilich's paper; other societies are mentioned only in passing. All of his informa-

---

28 *Ibid.,* p. 531.

tion about the Tikopia is drawn directly or indirectly from the work of Raymond Firth, who states quite flatly that the relationship between *HSA* and *HSF* is *positive:*

> In the normal way the father and the mother's brother of a child live in amity, the mother being the initial link between them, but the child forming the really vital social tie.[29]

The relationship between *HSF* and *HSA* when the former is the father and the latter is the maternal grandfather is a little more difficult to investigate and is affected by customs of residence, in-law avoidance, and the like, but even in societies in which a man avoids his father-in-law, it does not necessarily follow that he dislikes or fears him. If the society is patriarchal and has a favorite nephew pattern he may prefer his mother's brother's daughter to all other potential spouses. If he marries her, his lifelong *HSF* becomes his father-in-law and a potential *HSF* for his own son, which complicates matters.

Bureaucratic examples of the natural triad present similar problems. It is very doubtful that negative sentiments between warden and social worker or between line officer and chaplain are normal in their respective social systems, even though holders of these positions are likely to develop dissimilar attitudes. In many cases the prison social worker is directly subject to the warden's authority just as any army chaplain would report to the local commander. When and if such pairs of functionaries are organizationally independent, they are apt to practice a high degree of mutual avoidance since neither has anything to gain from a show of hostility.

In real life the natural triad is fairly uncommon. If *HSA* and *HSF* have *no* significant relationship and "a vacuous balance" is therefore achieved, there is no triad to be observed since, as Freilich says, "a triad consists of three roles intimately interlinked." The terms of the dyadic relationship between an uncle and his favorite nephew are clear enough and its expansion to a triad that includes the father is not obligatory. Indeed, if the father-son relationship is really negative and the uncle-nephew relationship is positive and the father holds jural authority over the son, both uncle and nephew have compelling reasons not to allow the development of a triad in which their coalition would be essentially helpless against their opponent.

Physical separation is one solution and secrecy is another. Pitts[30] describes the tendency of small children in the French bourgeois family

---

[29] Firth, *op. cit.*, p. 204.

[30] Jesse Pitts, "The Case of the French Bourgeoisie," in Rose Laub Coser, ed., *The Family: Its Structure and Functions* (New York: St. Martin's Press, Inc., 1954), pp. 545–50.

to seek preferential relationships with relatives within the extended family. These relationships are partly clandestine; they involve guilty secrets and imply a betrayal of the child's parents, but on occasion they are covertly encouraged by the parents in order to advance their own interests within the extended family.

The alternative of a solidary triad cannot be completely disregarded. In Tikopia, as in some other patripotestal societies, the authoritative father is not a brutal tyrant and the tensions he generates in managing his son do not prevent him from drinking and feasting with his son's uncle. The key to the puzzle may be the recognition that relationships involving authority cannot be automatically classified as hostile. Some are only ambivalent. Others are downright friendly.

VIII

THE MOTIVES
OF HAMLET

A great many dramatic situations can be cast in triadic form, since they involve the confrontation of a coalition and a closely related opponent. It remains to be seen whether analyzing a work of literature by means of triad theory contributes anything either to the theory or to our understanding of the drama.

Hamlet is an obvious choice for such an exercise, if only because of Shakespeare's explicit concern with the nature of human action: "For here lies the point:" says the Gravedigger, "if I drown myself wittingly, it argues an act; and an act hath three branches —it is to act, to do, and to perform." Although a distinguished Shakespearian critic once called the history of Hamlet criticism "a blot on the intellectual record of the race," [1] hardly any writer of the past two centuries with a theory of human motivation has resisted the temptation to try it out on this inexhaustible text. No other piece of writing has provoked half as many hypotheses. An anonymous German scholar is quoted as saying that every essay on *Hamlet* has a good part and a bad; in the good part the author refutes all previous theories; and in the bad part he presents his own.

[1] Elmer Edgar Stoll, "Hamlet: An Historical and Comparative Study," *Research Publications of the University of Minnesota*, VIII, No. 5 (September 1919).

By virtue of its depth and breadth, Hamlet criticism covers every conceivable aspect of the play. The rosters of the University of Wittenberg have been combed to show that several Rosenkrantzes and Gyldnstjernes were enrolled there in the seventeenth century. The view from Krönborg Castle at sunrise has been checked against the versions of the ghost scene in the First and Second Quartos. The customs governing the burial of suicides in Denmark have been scrutinized.[2] Every word in the saga of Amleth, written down by Saxo Grammaticus in the twelfth century and adapted by Belleforest in his *Histoires Tragiques* published in 1576, has been examined with exceeding care. Shakespeare's indebtedness to writings he might have read, such as Burton's *Anatomy of Melancholy* and Montaigne's *Apologie de Raimond Sebond* has been painstakingly parsed; and the influences of unknown works, like the lost Hamlet play possibly written by Thomas Kyd have been weighed with equal gravity.

More important for our present purpose, the personal relationships in *Hamlet* have been analyzed with a care unprecedented in literature or life. With regard to Hamlet's feelings about the Players, Claudius' sentiments towards Polonius, Ophelia's chastity, and the friendship between Hamlet and Horatio, every shred of evidence has been culled and compared, although, by some miracle, new evidence continues to be found, such as Wilson's recent discovery that the courtiers interpret the play-within-a-play as a threat by Hamlet to poison Claudius and not as a revelation of the elder Hamlet's murder.[3] The text is so fertile in such discoveries that some desperate critics have concluded that Shakespeare designed the play as an unsolvable puzzle.

The first scene, it will be remembered, takes place on the battlements of the royal castle. The sentries and Hamlet's friend Horatio see a ghost they recognize as Hamlet's father. The second scene introduces Claudius, the late King's brother, who has married Gertrude, the widowed Queen, and ascended the throne. Laertes, son of the King's minister Polonius, is given permission to return to France. Hamlet is chided for mourning his father too much and yields to the urging of the King and Queen not to return to school at Wittenberg. There follows the first soliloquy in which Hamlet complains about his mother's hasty and "incestuous" marriage with his uncle. He is interrupted by Horatio, who tells him about the ghost; they undertake to watch for it the same night. In the next scene, Laertes takes leave of his sister Ophelia and warns her against Hamlet's attentions. Their father, Polonius, overhearing the conversation,

---

2 Claud W. Sykes, "Alias William Shakespeare?" in C. C. H. Williamson, ed., *Readings on the Character of Hamlet* (London: George Allen & Unwin, 1950).

3 J. Dover Wilson, *What Happens in Hamlet* (Cambridge: The University Press, 1962).

questions her about Hamlet and orders her to break off all contact with him; she agrees to do so. The same night, on the sentries' platform, the Ghost appears again, telling Hamlet that Claudius poisoned him as he slept in his orchard and accusing Gertrude of indecent haste in marrying again and possibly of prior adultery with Claudius. He exhorts Hamlet to take revenge against Claudius, but warns him not to contrive anything against his mother. Hamlet swears his friends to absolute secrecy.

Between Acts I and II there is a lapse of time. As Act II opens, Polonius is sending a servant to spy upon Laertes' conduct in Paris. Then Ophelia enters to report that Hamlet, disordered in dress and appearance, had come to her room, stared, sighed, and gone away. Since her last appearance, she has rejected his letters and denied him access to her. Polonius goes to report the incident to the King.

The King and Queen receive Hamlet's old school fellows, Rosenkrantz and Guildenstern, who have been summoned to find out what afflicts Hamlet. Afterwards the King speaks with the Ambassadors returned from Norway. Polonius, showing the King a love letter from Hamlet to Ophelia, insists that Hamlet has been driven mad by Ophelia's coldness. A meeting between the lovers is arranged, with the King and Polonius hidden to overhear what is said. Hamlet baits Polonius in the fishmonger scene (according to one theory, because he has overheard the end of the previous conversation), then greets Rosenkrantz and Guildenstern, and makes them admit they have been sent for on his behalf. He learns that the "tragedians of the city" are on their way to Elsinore and presently they appear. At Hamlet's request, the First Player recites a long speech about the killing of Priam by Pyrrhus and the frenzy of Hecuba and the Players agree to stage a play called "The Murther of Gonzago" for the entertainment of the Court and to insert some new lines in it.

Hamlet is left alone for a long soliloquy in which he contrasts the Player's simulated grief for Hecuba with his own silence about his father, then reminds himself that he has no evidence against his uncle except the testimony of the Ghost who "may be a devil," and explains his plan to have the Players re-enact a murder similar to that of his father so that he can watch Claudius' reaction. Rosenkrantz and Guildenstern report to the King and Queen that they have not learned much from Hamlet and they convey his invitation to the play.

Meanwhile, the stage is set for Ophelia's meeting with Hamlet, spied on by the King and Polonius. Hamlet appears, delivers his famous soliloquy on suicide, and greets Ophelia, who begins the interview by returning his presents and complaining of unkindness. Hamlet upbraids her harshly and somewhat enigmatically. The King, convinced that Hamlet is neither in love nor mad, decides to send him away to England. Then,

Polonius plans another interview, this one to be between Hamlet and the Queen, with himself concealed.

Hamlet briefs the Players on their evening's performance—and on the art of acting. He enlists Horatio to help watch Claudius at the critical moment so that later they may compare notes. As the play-within-a-play begins, there is more conversation among the principals, then a dumb show which recapitulates the murder of a king in a garden by a man who takes the crown for himself and seduces the queen. One of the major enigmas of *Hamlet* is that Claudius is unmoved by this almost literal re-enactment of his crime. The play-within-a-play proceeds. The Player Queen assures her husband in extravagant terms that she would not consider remarriage if he died. The real King and Queen are not seriously perturbed until "one Lucianus, nephew to the King" enters among the Players and begins to brew a vegetable poison. At this point, the King rises, Polonius stops the performance, and the entire Court sweeps away leaving Hamlet and Horatio behind. They agree that the Ghost's story has been verified. Almost at once, Rosenkrantz and Guildenstern return to say that the King is "marvelous distempered" and that Hamlet's mother has sent for him. Hamlet teases them mercilessly.

Rosenkrantz and Guildenstern are ordered to take Hamlet away to England. Left alone, the King attempts to pray and also tells the audience that the Ghost's accusations are true. Hamlet enters unseen, considers attacking Claudius but forbears to do it lest he send the King to Heaven by killing him "in the purging of his soul, when he is fit and seasoned for his passage." He then goes to his mother's chamber where Polonius has just hidden himself. Hamlet's entrance is so menacing that the Queen calls for help, Polonius echoes her cry, and Hamlet runs him through with a sword. Without much further attention to Polonius, he scolds the Queen for exchanging his father for his uncle. And although she seems remorseful, Hamlet's fury increases. The Ghost appears again, in a nightgown, visible to Hamlet but not to the Queen, and reminds Hamlet to whet his "almost blunted purpose" and in effect to be nicer to his mother. Hamlet continues to scold Gertrude but in a calm and reasonable tone to which she seems receptive. He urges her to break with Claudius: "Good night—but go not to my uncle's bed," and instructs her not to reveal that his madness is assumed. This much, at least, Gertrude promises, and they part on good terms, Hamlet tugging the corpse of Polonius towards the exit.

After an interlude of gruesome hide-and-seek the body is found, and Hamlet is shipped off to England in the custody of Rosenkrantz and Guildenstern, who carry secret letters ordering the English to execute him. As they depart, Hamlet encounters the Norwegian army on its way to an unnecessary war and contrasts "The imminent death of twenty thousand men /That for a fantasy and trick of fame /Go to their graves" with the slow progress of his own revenge.

Back at Elsinore, Ophelia goes mad and Laertes returns from France to raise a rebellion. He breaks in on the King and Queen and demands satisfaction for his father's death. The King calms him, deflects his anger to Hamlet, and promises to assist in his revenge. Meanwhile Horatio learns from a letter that Hamlet has escaped from his convoy and has returned to Denmark. The King has just begun to plot with Laertes when another letter announces Hamlet's imminent arrival. Then the King and Laertes plan the fencing match at which Hamlet is to be killed by a poisoned foil and a poisoned drink. They learn of Ophelia's drowning in the brook.

Act V begins with two clowns amusing each other with jokes and songs as they dig Ophelia's grave. Hamlet enters with Horatio, asks curious questions and discovers the unearthed skull of Yorick. His reflections on mortality are interrupted by the arrival of Ophelia's funeral procession, Laertes and Hamlet grapple in the grave and then Hamlet storms off. He tells Horatio how he had found the King's commission and had forged another ordering the immediate execution of Rosenkrantz and Guildenstern on their arrival in England. A courtier brings him Laertes' challenge to a fencing match attended by the King, Queen, "and all the State." The match begins. The King sets out the poisoned cup. Hamlet is winning when Laertes wounds him with the poisoned weapon, but in the scuffle they exchange rapiers and Laertes is poisoned also. The Queen drinks the poisoned wine and dies, Laertes confesses his treachery, Hamlet stabs the King and forces the rest of the wine down his throat. Thus all the principals die, except for Horatio who remains alive to tell the story. Fortinbras comes in and Hamlet is eulogized.

Although there are more than two dozen speaking parts in Hamlet and all the minor personages are well-rounded, interpretation, like the play itself, fixes upon the central figure of the Prince. Most conceptions of him fall into three categories—the sick hero, the healthy hero, and the nonhero.[4]

Hamlet's illness is usually traced back to Henry Mackenzie, who wrote about 1789. This early criticism described Hamlet's illness as not very grave, although, according to Mackenzie, Hamlet shows "some temporary marks of a real disorder" and the delicacy of his feelings towards Ophelia approaches weakness.[5] In *Wilhelm Meister's Apprenticeship,* which first appeared in 1796, Hamlet's condition was described thus:

4 Omitting a category of wider surmises, as that Hamlet was a woman or a symbol of the Roman Catholic Church.

5 Henry Mackenzie, quoted in Williamson, *op. cit.,* pp. 24–27.

A lovely, pure, noble, and most moral nature, without the strength of nerve which forms a hero, seeks to meet a burden which it cannot bear and must not pass away. All duties are holy for him; the present is too hard. Impossibilities have been required of him; not in themselves impossibilities, but such for him. He winds, and turns, and torments himself; he advances and recoils; is ever put in mind, ever puts himself in mind; at last does all but lose his purpose from his thoughts; yet still without recovering his peace of mind.[6]

This became the prevailing stage interpretation in the following century, and the sweet, nervous Hamlet, high-mindedly moping from one soliloquy to the next, is still with us.

At the end of the nineteenth century the patient took a turn for the worse. The magisterial Bradley, professor of poetry in the University of Oxford, diagnosed Hamlet as catatonic:

. . . all this, and whatever else passed in a sickening round through Hamlet's mind, was not the healthy and right deliberation of a man with such task, but otiose thinking hardly deserving the name of thought, an unconscious weaving of pretexts for inaction, aimless tossings on a sick bed. . . .[7]

From this it was only a short step to Freud's Hamlet, a neurotic "able to do anything except take vengeance on the man who did away with his father and took that father's place with his mother, the man who shows him the repressed wishes of his own childhood realized." [8] Freud was also quite sure that *Hamlet* reflected the poet's own experience, discovering that it was written soon after the deaths of Shakespeare's father and his young son, Hamnet, although later Freud "ceased to believe that the author of Shakespeare's works was the man from Stratford." [9] A much more elaborate psychoanalytic version was developed by Ernest Jones.[10]

In the measured judgment of T. S. Eliot, author of *The Cocktail Party* and other notable works for the stage, Shakespeare failed entirely with *Hamlet* because he undertook a subject too difficult for his talents.[11]

Hamlet the healthy hero has had a longer, less complex history. Stoll, who brought a great deal of factual evidence to the feverish world of

[6] Johann Wolfgang von Goethe, *Wilhelm Meister's Apprenticeship*, trans. Thomas Carlyle (New York: Collier Books, 1962), p. 236.

[7] A. C. Bradley, *Shakespearian Tragedy* (New York: The Macmillan Company, 1949), p. 123 (orig. pub. 1904).

[8] Sigmund Freud, *The Interpretation of Dreams*, trans. James Strachey (London: The Hogarth Press, Ltd., 1958), p. 65 (orig. pub. 1900).

[9] *Ibid.*, fn., p. 266.

[10] See his *Essays in Applied Psychoanalysis* (London and Vienna: International Psycho-analytical Press, 1923).

[11] T. S. Eliot, "Hamlet," in *Selected Essays* (New York: Harcourt, Brace & World, Inc., 1950), pp. 121–26.

Hamlet criticism,[12] showed that Hamlet was universally perceived to be a noble, gallant, and admirable figure for nearly two hundred years after the play first appeared. Popular and literary opinion found nothing wrong with Hamlet until the rise of romanticism. A comparison with other revenge plays of the sixteenth century suggests that the delayed execution of the revenge was an essential convention (otherwise there could be no play). The self-reproaches of the hero are equally conventional, reminding the audience that he takes his task seriously and does not lose sight of it during the postponements around which the dramatic action is staged. According to this interpretation, Hamlet has no real grounds for self-reproach. None of the other characters describe him as weak, timorous, or cowardly. The closing speeches—the author's opportunity to summarize—praise Hamlet more highly than any other Shakespearian hero. The peals of artillery at the end do not call to mind a frightened invalid. Stoll demonstrates by many Elizabethan examples that Hamlet's reluctance to kill the King at prayer lest he send his soul to Heaven was a perfectly normal sentiment for an Elizabethan audience which would have been accustomed to the idea that revenge—at least stage revenge—should be directed against both body and soul. This is probably the crucial point in the choice between a morbid and a wholesome Hamlet, and we shall return to it a little later.

With the characteristic tendency of Hamlet criticism to fall into excesses, the twentieth-century revival of the healthy hero has led to such views as those of Grebanier,[13] whose Hamlet is so faultless that Ophelia must be presented as a psychopath to account for the trouble between them, and to the more intricate opinion of Dover Wilson [14] that Hamlet suffers from a mild type of emotional disorder while feigning a more serious syndrome. If Hamlet is given a clean bill of health, the play's mystery is shifted to the other characters. Does Polonius feign his dotage or is he really senile? Do the Ghost's passing references to adultery prove that Gertrude and Claudius had an affair before the murder? If so, how did the Ghost find out about it after his death?

An even greater effect of novelty can be achieved by making Hamlet the villain of the play. In Knight's *Wheel of Fire* Hamlet "is not of flesh or blood, he is a spirit of penetrating intellect and cynicism and misery, without faith in himself or anyone else, murdering his love of Ophelia, on the brink of insanity, taking delight in cruelty, torturing Claudius, breaking his mother's heart, a poison in the midst of the healthy bustle of the Court." In this fascinating version, Claudius, "a man kindly, con-

12 Stoll, *op. cit.*

13 Bernard Grebanier, *The Heart of Hamlet: The Play Shakespeare Wrote* (New York: Thomas Y. Crowell Company, 1960).

14 Wilson, *op. cit.*

fident, and fond of pleasure," courteous and dignified, a "true leader," is the hero. "Claudius, as he appears in the play, is not a criminal. He is—strange as it may seem—a good and gentle King, enmeshed by the chain of causality linking him with his crime. And this chain, he might, perhaps, have broken except for Hamlet, and all would have been well." [15]

For Salvador de Madariaga, Hamlet (whom he turns into a Spaniard with as little hesitation as that Herr Professor Borne who wrote "Hamlet *is* Germany") is a ruthless, egotistical killer on the model of Cesare Borgia. Less reputable scholars have revealed that the Prince was a syphilitic, a homosexual, or an impostor like Mark Twain's Pauper.

It should be interesting to see whether triad theory kindles any new light here. The record exists to warn us against the dangers of taking the play too literally or not literally enough.

Triad theory deals with the tactical constraints that develop in every situation involving contention. The formation of a winning coalition in a triad is an attempt to halt contention by establishing peace within the coalition and securely subjugating the opponent, but this purpose cannot be accomplished as long as the opponent has some hope of luring either of the partners out of the existing coalition and into a new coalition with himself.

Suppose we think of Hamlet as a living man and visualize his problem in tactical terms. There is never any question of his ability to gain access to Claudius and stab him. Except for one passing reference, Shakespeare eliminated the Swiss guards who protected the King in earlier versions of the story. Let us suppose, then, that Hamlet had left the Ghost's presence to march to the King and cut his throat forthwith. As many commentators have pointed out, this would have dispensed with most of the play. And as Hamlet says, the Ghost's testimony is not conclusive:

> The spirit that I have seen
> May be a devil, and the devil hath power
> T'assume a pleasing shape, and perhaps
> Out of my weakness and my melancholy,
> As he is very potent with such spirits,
> Abuses me to damn me.

But these difficulties aside, we have only to imagine the aftermath of that decisive, unhesitating act to take most of the mystery out of Hamlet's indecision. Let us remember that there is no shred of demonstrable evidence to support the Ghost's story, and none is obtainable. The text seems to tell us that Gertrude is ignorant of the elder Hamlet's murder.

[15] G. Wilson Knight, *The Wheel of Fire: Interpretation of Shakespeare's Tragedy* (Cleveland: World Publishing Company, 1963), pp. 34, 35, and 38 (orig. pub. 1930).

So far as Hamlet—or the audience—can determine, there is no chance that witnesses to the crime will ever come forward. The exotic mode of poisoning [16] precludes a proof by autopsy. Hamlet, so far as he knows, will never be able to demonstrate to an impartial observer that his father was murdered or that Claudius was the murderer. In fact, Hamlet never *does* obtain any direct evidence about the murder. Claudius' reaction to the play-within-a-play is sufficient to convince Hamlet, and perhaps Horatio as well; it would hardly satisfy a jury. The commission issued to Rosenkrantz and Guildenstern to have Hamlet put to death in England provides him with demonstrable grounds for taking revenge on his own account, and the King's effort to poison Hamlet by one means or another lends support to the tale that Horatio eventually unfolds to the survivors. But if we did not have Claudius' confession in the prayer scene—addressed only to Heaven and the audience—there would be as much uncertainty about the murder of the elder Hamlet as now remains about Gertrude's adultery. Hamlet never entertains the hope that Claudius will make a public confession.

Hamlet's tactical problem is how to take his revenge on Claudius without himself being punished as a murderer. Were he to kill Claudius after the initial appearance of the Ghost or when he found him at prayer he could hardly hope to escape with his own life. To the Court of Elsinore and to the unseen populace whose presence is felt throughout the play the act would be abhorrent—regicide, almost parricide—a horror not to be excused or understood. Revenge for his father's murder is the only motive that might extenuate such a crime, keep Hamlet's life and honor intact, and leave him free to ascend the throne.

But it is unlikely that Hamlet's mere assertion would convince the onlookers of Claudius' guilt. And the evidence he might present would seem ridiculous—the testimony of a phantom, the King's boredom at a palace entertainment. The corroboration of Horatio—Hamlet's friend and follower—would be plainly worthless. There is only one witness whose testimony might save Hamlet after he killed Claudius, and whose opposition after the same event would certainly be his undoing. Hamlet's sole hope of surviving an act of revenge is to win his mother's support, or at least her neutrality. And this, to my mind, is the central action of the play—the contention within the Claudius-Gertrude-Hamlet triad as Hamlet attempts to dissolve the coalition of Claudius and Gertrude against himself.

Hamlet's role begins with a conversation among all three of them and

[16] Modern nit-picking has identified the poison as the alkaloid hyoscine in the plant *Hyoscyamus niger* and has pronounced the method of administering it plausible, although apparently untested.

ends in the same way. The initial power distribution is displayed in their first scene together as the King "beseeches" and the Queen "prays" Hamlet to give up his intention of going back to school in Wittenberg. Both of them seem to recognize that he is free to refuse. Hamlet ignores the King but yields to his mother's wish. At this time Claudius is more than affable—"be as ourself in Denmark"—and he celebrates Hamlet's decision by formal carousing and salutes of artillery.

There is no doubt for the moment that Claudius, the anointed King, is stronger than Hamlet, but the manner of his election is not very clear and research into the constitution of medieval Denmark does not help much. There seems to have been an elective procedure at one time, but the King's eldest son was generally the sole candidate, and, in any case, it is not certain that Shakespeare had the Danish constitution in mind. During his first appearance, Claudius refers to Gertrude as "Th'imperial jointress to this warlike state," suggesting that he—and possibly the elder Hamlet as well—held the crown through Gertrude, as did some husbands of English and Scottish queens. There is also a frank announcement that the councilors have played a part in arranging the succession, "nor have we herein barred your better wisdoms, which have freely gone with this affair along." Later on there will be repeated hints that public opinion has not entirely accepted the election of Claudius. Throughout the play Hamlet is, among other things, the potential leader of a coup d'état, and this may be why he is addressed with such circumspection by Claudius and Gertrude. Laertes, warning Ophelia about Hamlet's intentions, speaks of him as though he were already King:

> . . . his will is not his own;
> For he himself is subject to his birth.
> He may not, as unvalued persons do,
> Carve for himself, for on his choice depends
> The safety and health of this whole state
> And therefore must his choice be circumscrib'd
> Unto the voice and yielding of that body
> Whereof he is the head.

The King pursues his investigation of Hamlet's affliction with a growing suspicion that Hamlet threatens him and his crown. One modern scholar [17] attaches extraordinary importance to Hamlet's remark that the murderer in the play-within-a-play is "one Lucianus, nephew to the King," interpreting this as a thinly veiled threat against Claudius' life by Hamlet, his nephew. Upon hearing the remark, the King loses no time in sending Rosenkrantz and Guildenstern back to Hamlet for further

17 J. Dover Wilson, *op. cit.*

information, and this time Hamlet openly declares that he wants the crown.

> Hamlet: Sir, I lack advancement.
> Rosenkrantz: How can that be, when you have the voice of the King himself for your succession in Denmark?
> Hamlet: Ay, sir, but "while the grass grows"—the proverb is something musty.[18]

When this report is brought to Claudius, he mutters about his personal safety and begins to draft Hamlet's travel orders. After the death of Polonius, the King's apprehension of danger is even stronger, but he still speaks to Hamlet with circumspect politeness, and reminds his followers that Hamlet enjoys too much popular support to be attacked directly: "yet must not be put the strong laws on him; he's loved of the distracted multitude." Claudius is even more explicit about Hamlet's political strength in explaining to Laertes why Hamlet was not accused of murdering Polonius: "the other motive /Why to a public count I might not go /Is the great love the general gender bear him."

All that the King dares to do is hasten Hamlet's departure to England and secretly command his execution there. This attempt on his life becomes the fourth count in Hamlet's private indictment of Claudius, the first three being the murder of his father, the seduction of his mother, and the usurpation of the crown that should have been his.

> He that hath kill'd my king, and whor'd my mother;
> Popp'd in between th'election and my hopes;
> Thrown out his angle for my proper life,
> And with such coz'nage—is't not perfect conscience
> To quit him with this arm?

In the last scene of the play, Hamlet, dying, nominates Fortinbras to succeed him, as if he had always been the rightful King. As the play closes, Fortinbras reflects that "he was likely had he been put on, /To have prov'd most royally."

Until the play-within-a-play, Claudius and Gertrude always confront Hamlet together and they speak with one voice, although with delicate differences of tone which tell us that Gertrude is genuinely concerned about her son while Claudius fears him. Nevertheless, they act jointly— urging Hamlet to stay at Court, sending for Rosenkrantz and Guildenstern, testing Polonius' theory that Hamlet is distracted by love, accepting the invitation to the play-within-a-play, and arranging the interview that follows it. Shakespeare clearly intends them to be a coalition whenever they face Hamlet. Business that does not involve the Prince, such

---

[18] "While the grass grows, the horse starves."

as Laertes' petition and the negotiations with Norway, is handled by the King alone.

We begin, then, with a Type 5 triad in which Claudius is *A*, Gertrude is *B*, and Hamlet is *C*. The *AB* coalition, Claudius and Gertrude, dominates Hamlet easily, but a *BC* coalition, Gertrude and Hamlet, might be able to dominate Claudius. Hamlet's only way of accomplishing his revenge and surviving afterwards would be to persuade Gertrude to desert Claudius and draw her into a coalition with himself. The aftermath of his revenge would be largely determined by her reaction to this strategy. Hamlet can scarcely hope to escape punishment or seize the crown if his own mother accuses him of unprovoked regicide, which is precisely the reaction to be expected from her because of her solidary coalition with Claudius. Hamlet, melancholy and considering suicide as an escape, rails at himself as "a rogue and peasant slave" and "a dull and muddy-mettled rascal," but the act to which the Ghost urges him is impracticable until he can find some means of luring his mother out of the conservative coalition which renders him helpless to accomplish his revenge without losing his honor or leaving the ultimate advantage with Claudius.

The situation as it presents itself initially to Hamlet is bleak. He has trouble enough convincing himself of the Ghost's veracity and no hope of finding enough evidence to convince his mother. In addition, he suspects Gertrude of complicity in Claudius' crime, in which case, proof would be irrelevant and his chance of disrupting the coalition would be even slimmer.

Hamlet is unjust to Gertrude in at least two respects (perhaps because of his well-known oedipus complex). First, insofar as the audience can tell, she has not been an accomplice to the murder of Hamlet's father, knows nothing about it, and probably never finds out. Hamlet's accusation—just after he has stabbed Polonius—passes by her quite unnoticed:

Queen: O, what a rash and bloody deed is this!
Hamlet: A bloody deed—almost as bad, good mother,
         As kill a king, and marry with his brother.
Queen: As kill a king?
Hamlet: Ay, lady, it was my word.

She pays no attention whatever. A moment later she is still asking, "What have I done that thou dar'st wag thy tongue /In noise so rude against me?" Hamlet, abandoning the accusation of complicity in the murder, continues by complaining of her second marriage and her love for Claudius, but although he calls Claudius a murderer and a usurper, he does not mention adultery in his tirade.

Hamlet also seems to underestimate his mother's attachment to him, of which Claudius is so acutely aware. Even after he and Hamlet have fallen into open enmity, Claudius still feigns paternal tenderness in Gertrude's presence, and says to Laertes, "the Queen his mother /Lives almost by his looks."

By the time Hamlet goes to see his mother, the configuration of the triad has changed. Claudius knows—if Hamlet does not—that by com- missioning Rosenkrantz and Guildenstern to arrange Hamlet's death, he has abandoned his coalition with Gertrude, who can never be ex- pected to concur in her son's assassination. In the very next scene he accepts Polonius' offer to spy on Gertrude and Hamlet.

On his way to his mother's closet, Hamlet sees Claudius at prayer, draws his sword, but then hesitates and passes on. This scene certainly permits indecision to be taken as the theme of the play, no matter how plausible Hamlet's refusal to take the King at his spiritual best [19] may have appeared to Elizabethan audiences. Since the preceding scene, Hamlet has been rationally certain of Claudius' guilt, and just before his entrance, the last doubts of the audience are dispelled by the solil- oquy in which Claudius confesses the murder. But I cannot find in Ham- let's hesitation the neurotic self-doubt that some critics have discerned, for he sounds almost arrogantly confident as he finishes with, "This physic but prolongs thy sickly days," and goes on his way to see his mother. At this point Hamlet does not yet suspect that Claudius is plot- ting against him or that the Claudius-Gertrude coalition is beginning to dissolve.

Whether Gertrude has an inkling of these changes is uncertain. In the next scene she enters with Polonius, who advises her how to deal with Hamlet. We do not know if the advice is welcome. She tells him to with- draw and he hides behind the arras. We do not know from the text whether this is done with her knowledge, although the scene is usually played as if it were. Hamlet's main concern after he has killed Polonius is that the interview not be interrupted. He finds his mother un- expectedly receptive to his long tirade:

> O Hamlet, speak no more!
> Thou turn'st mine eyes into my very soul,
> And there I see such black and grained spots
> As will not leave their tinct.

When the Ghost leaves, Hamlet urges his mother to separate from Claudius and to form a coalition with himself. He warns her not to report their conversation to Claudius and especially not to reveal "That

[19] Hamlet expresses a related sentiment in his very first appearance when he laments his mother's wedding without suspecting Claudius of anything more than undue haste: "Would I had met my dearest foe in heaven /Or ever I had seen that day, Horatio!"

I essentially am not in madness, /But mad in craft." Her interests, he says in a complex metaphor, are the same as his own, and she will destroy herself if she violates his confidences. Gertrude agrees and swears silence; the rest of their talk is affectionate. She keeps her word and tells the King that Hamlet is raving mad, has killed Polonius in a fit, and grieves insanely over the body. Here Gertrude acts in concert with Hamlet against Claudius, and thereafter, so far as can be deduced from her few remaining speeches, she supports Hamlet quietly while Claudius plans Hamlet's assassination, first with Rosenkrantz and Guildenstern and then with the furious Laertes. Gertrude never supports Claudius again, except briefly when Laertes breaks in at the head of a mob. When, at the fencing match, she drinks the poisoned cup by mistake and is dying, her last words are directed to "my dear Hamlet."

Although Hamlet scolds himself in one more soliloquy ("How all occasions do inform against me /And spur my dull revenge!"), he blames himself for delay, not indecision. There is no remaining trace of indecision in that speech or in any of his subsequent actions. After the interview with his mother, he is never again presented with an opportunity to kill the King until the last scene when he does so. But he shows no inner conflict, and he tells Horatio convincingly that he intends to do the deed before the news about Rosenkrantz and Guildenstern arrives from England. The crushing weight of the Claudius-Gertrude coalition has been lifted from him. The documentary evidence he brings back— the King's secret commission to have him killed in England—will justify his rebellion to the Court and, for somewhat different reasons, to Gertrude. When Hamlet gives his dying instructions to Horatio and nominates Fortinbras for the vacant throne, he still shows the assurance that has marked all his actions since the interview with his mother—his easy contemptuous handling of Rosenkrantz and Guildenstern, his cheerful return to Elsinore, his behavior at the graveyard, and his quarrel and reconciliation with Laertes.

If Gertrude is almost speechless throughout the latter half of the play, it is because there is almost nothing she can say either to Claudius, her deserted partner, or to Hamlet, with whom she is now unhappily allied in the accomplishment of her own ruin. "Wretched Queen adieu," he says, but saves the remaining minutes of his life for Horatio and Fortinbras.

IX

FULL-FLEDGED
GAMES

It may be useful at this point to examine the triads that form in offices and factories. These are very diverse, and sometimes a little difficult to pick out of a large web of activities and technical relationships. They may not be immediately apparent in a hierarchy having seven or eight levels of rank or in a work group with a half dozen technical specialties. It is only by close observation and analysis that we can rediscover the familiar types of triads in these apparently complex situations.

Certain triadic patterns appear repeatedly under different guises. Almost every sizable work force can be divided into managers, supervisors, and workers. All bureaucracies contain the triads composed of a superior, a subordinate, and a staff functionary, the two-level triads of a superior and two subordinates or two superiors and a subordinate, and hierarchical triads composed of a superior, a subordinate, and *his* subordinate. Since large organizations have a variety of outside contacts, there is an entire species of triads composed of either two members and an outsider or two outsiders and a member. In organizations that value seniority the triad of veteran, short-service worker, and recruit may be significant, especially when it is associated with differences in skill. Traces of the medieval triad of master-journeyman-apprentice still persist in the skilled trades and in some of the professions.

The triads found in large organizations differ in some ways from those that develop in families and other primary groups, the most striking difference being that in the large organization the members of a triad may be collectivities. Some triads are made up of both individual and collective actors, for instance all the maintenance men in a plant may interact as a collectivity with the chief engineer, on one hand, and the foreman, on the other.

Triads in large organizations often have a representative and repetitive character because of the proximity of collective actors. A single manager, supervisor, and worker may behave at times as representatives of the groups to which they belong so that they compose a miniature replica of the triad of collectivities from which they draw many of their attitudes and assumptions. When this occurs, even imperfectly, there will be many triads that interact and form coalitions in similar fashion.

The representative character of triads in large organizations is often emphasized by the presence of spectators who are interested in the triadic relationships around them because they themselves will be affected by any gains or losses in the relative power of their associates. The formation of coalitions in large organizations is thus characterized by a certain interchangeability, not only because individuals represent their groups, but also because the substitutability of actors is an essential feature of large-scale organizations, in which patterns of interaction must not be disrupted when individuals are replaced for one reason or another.

Status schisms, which are found in most large organizations, divide the membership into nonoverlapping categories such as officers and enlisted men, executives and workers, and clergy and laity. A status schism establishes a formal discontinuity in power, privilege, and social personality between an upper stratum and a lower stratum, so that no member of the lower stratum can be equal or superior to any member of the upper stratum under normal circumstances. A status schism is maintained by rules that limit the amount, the form, and the content of interaction between the two groups and that assert the superiority of the upper stratum in any interaction with members of the lower stratum.

Obviously, mixed coalitions are discouraged. In the military service, for example, coalitions between officers and enlisted men are prohibited by certain regulations and by military customs. In practice, the ban on mixed coalitions against an officer opponent is much more effective than the ban on mixed coalitions against an enlisted opponent, since coalitions of the latter kind do not threaten the dominance of the upper stratum.

THE FUNDAMENTAL DILEMMA IN COALITION FORMATION

When we analyzed coalitions in the nuclear family, we discovered a fundamental contradiction between the impulse to form winning coalitions and the desire for a like partner and an unlike opponent. In the nuclear family almost all winning coalitions involve partners who are unlike in generation or gender and opponents who resemble at least one partner in one of these fundamental ways. Likeness of generation between husband and wife is a claim for solidarity against the generations above and below; likeness of gender between mother and daughter is an equally valid claim. But the only configurations in the nuclear family that satisfy the condition of like partners against an unlike opponent are the coalition of two brothers against a mother or sister or of two sisters against a father or brother—coalitions which are seldom profitable. Despite the ingenuity of a thousand tribes in devising different forms of the family, every form is beset with conflict and uncertainty.

Any organization with more than two levels in its status hierarchy faces a similar dilemma which can be only partly overcome by status schisms and other devices for keeping unsuitable coalition partners apart. The essence of this dilemma is that the coalitions formed in hierarchical three-level triads, whether they are conservative coalitions that get the business of the organization done or revolutionary coalitions that defend the personal interests of the members, are incompatible with peer-group solidarity. Figure 9–1 shows a hierarchical triad ABC and next to it a peer of A labeled A'. Suppose a conservative coalition AB is formed within the triad. As soon as the triad ABA' is activated, the AB coalition will be incompatible with the coalition of the peers A and A'. The two coalitions cannot both be maintained unless B is rigorously segregated from A', so that the triad ABA' is prevented from forming at all. To achieve this condition throughout an organization it would be necessary to separate vertical interaction from horizontal interaction entirely, which would be inconceivable in most organizations.

Suppose that A, forced to choose between the incompatible coalitions AB and AA', chooses A'. In so doing A would eliminate himself as a coalition partner for B or C in any linked hierarchical triad. Regardless of the power distribution in the triad ABC, the formation of a BC coalition then becomes likely. Depending on the power distribution it may be either conservative or revolutionary, but in either case it will interfere with the formation of a coalition between B and *his* peer B' or C and *his* peer C'.

The dilemma is unresolvable except under highly unusual conditions. In general, the members of an organizational hierarchy must choose

FIGURE 9–1

The Choice Between Peer Coalitions and a Superior-Subordinate Coalition in a Hierarchical Triad

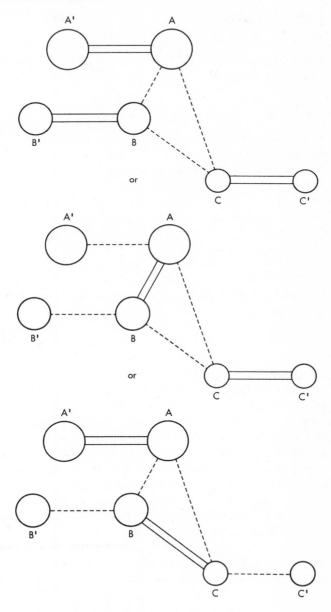

between vertical and horizontal solidarity. The kind of vertical solidarity offered to each participant depends upon the power distributions within the hierarchical triads to which he belongs and the kind of horizontal solidarity offered depends upon the number and proximity of peers. This choice is complicated by the interplay between coalition processes involving individuals and those involving collectivities. Peer groups formed by individual choice often become the actors in larger triads composed of collectivities.

COALITIONS IN A PUBLIC ENTERPRISE

The problems of coalition formation in large organizations are admirably illustrated in Crozier's study of an industrial monopoly created by the government of France.[1] This agency has thirty manufacturing plants and a number of additional facilities dispersed throughout the country. Each plant employs about 400 people, divided into managers, supervisors, and workers. The managers include a director and an assistant director, both graduates of the École Polytechnique, a technical engineer and a small administrative force headed by a comptroller. The supervisors are shop foremen and inspectors who are recruited through a general competitive examination. The workers are divided into two categories: semi-skilled production workers, mostly women, and highly skilled maintenance workers, all men.

The salient feature of this enterprise is that all employees, whatever their rank, have civil service tenure. They cannot be punished or rewarded in any significant way by supervisors or managers, and all job allocations are made according to a strict seniority system. Since production and marketing are highly routinized, there are relatively few managerial decisions to be made. There is correspondingly little scope for the supervisors, who maintain production records, keep track of expenditures and supplies, and make up daily schedules. They exercise little personal authority over the workers. The relationship between supervisors and workers, says the investigator, is "good but unimportant." [2] It is marked by mutual tolerance and indifference. A strong, active union places further checks on any authoritarian impulses a foreman may have.

The most contented group on the shop floor are the maintenance men, each of whom is responsible for the setting and repair of a small group of machines in a particular shop. He reports not to the foreman of that shop but to the technical engineer in charge of maintenance for the entire plant. Machine stoppages, which are frequent and unpredictable, are

[1] Michel Crozier, *The Bureaucratic Phenomenon* (Chicago: University of Chicago Press, 1964), Pt. II.
[2] *Ibid.*, p. 91.

the principal source of uncertainty in this highly routine operation, since the workers are penalized by loss of production if the stoppage is brief and by assignment to other duties if it is prolonged. Only the maintenance man assigned to a particular machine can cope with a breakdown for even if the foreman is competent to make repairs, he is prevented from doing so by the regulations. The maintenance men are not classified as supervisors but they are able to reward and punish "their" workers more readily than the foremen. The attitude of maintenance men to workers is one of good-humored contempt. The workers must try to get along with the maintenance men. The foremen, with a few exceptions, detest the maintenance men and find it depressing to observe them. The maintenance men, in a cheerful way, return the antagonism.

Above the shop level are the four members of the management team—a director in general charge, an assistant director responsible for production, a technical engineer responsible for maintenance, and a comptroller responsible for purchasing, inventory, and personnel administration. They belong to three entirely separate occupational corps with different career patterns. The assistant director, if he remains with the Monopoly, will be promoted to director by the simple operation of seniority, after he has obtained experience in two or three plants. The director, therefore, was necessarily an assistant director before assuming his present post. The technical engineer must expect to remain in the same plant and more or less at the same rank throughout his career. He has no colleagues in his own category and few opportunities for contact with his peers at other plants but, because of his responsibility for equipment, buildings, and machinery, and his direct supervision of the maintenance men, his vertical associations throughout the plant are more extensive than any other individual's. The comptroller belongs to still another corps; his duties are important but entirely routine, and he has little opportunity to influence operations.

These four men together form an advisory council which may or may not meet regularly. The director, assistant director, and comptroller belong to the council ex officio, but the technical engineer must be appointed to it. The comptroller reports to the director, although he is independently accountable for some transactions. The assistant director reports to the director, and the technical engineer is theoretically, but not actually, subordinate to the assistant director. All foremen report to the assistant director. The director has the ultimate responsibility for organizational performance but, except with regard to remodeling and new construction, he is not allowed to depart from the highly detailed operating procedures outlined by the Central Office.

One consequence of these rigid arrangements is that the same positions, with the same formal relationships, appear in all of the Monopoly's plants throughout the country. Since twenty plants were included in Crozier's study, he was able to observe the repeated appearance of certain coalitions.

He is careful to point out that the power distribution alone will not account for the coalitions observed; the content of each actor's role must also be considered:

> If our four players had the same stakes and commitments and no differences in roles, we could predict the formation of coalitions according to their respective powers. However, the problem is not so simple, because of the interplay of many more factors and the interference of another variable, the type of participation or commitment of the players to the game.[3]

In the twenty plants studied there were sixteen clear-cut cases of conflict between the technical engineer on the one hand and the assistant director and/or the director on the other. The four exceptions seem to confirm the rule. In one instance the technical engineer had succeeded in dominating the director; in another, he had suffered a neurotic collapse. In the two remaining cases, the plants were undergoing extensive renovation and the authority of the assistant directors had been temporarily enlarged as a result.

These organizations were clearly designed with the objective of removing the usual grounds of industrial conflict. Since coalitions are formed for purposes of conflict, the elimination of conflict ought to result in the elimination of coalitions as well.

The career lines of the several groups within the enterprise are segregated so that movement from one group to another is impossible. Authority over work procedures is centered in an inaccessible central office. The motives of ambition and power are meant to be neutralized by the absence of any opportunities for improving one's own status or reforming the system.

To a large extent, these "utopian" objectives are realized.[4] Conflict is rare and many of the usual coalition choices do not have to be made. The supervisors in these plants are not torn between conflicting allegiances; they are not caught in the middle. Although the foremen are close to the workers in attitudes and sentiments, there is no semblance of a coalition between them. Coalitions among the managers are also unknown, with the exception of the coalition occasionally formed between a director and an assistant director against a technical engineer.

The reduction of conflict does not result in an end to all trouble. Crozier describes a climate of vague hostility, low morale, resentment, and widespread dissatisfaction with the weak chain of command. The elimination of external problems seems to generate psychological problems for

3 *Ibid.*, p. 117.

4 For a description of a comparable situation in a private enterprise, see Alan Harrington, *Life in the Crystal Palace* (New York: Alfred A. Knopf, Inc., 1959).

many of the participants. The impossibility of getting ahead, the difficulty of making changes, and the dilution of responsibility are painful to those individuals who are not willing to make sacrifices for the sake of peaceful conformity.

There is one flaw in their utopian design around which conflict develops and coalitions are formed. The weak spot appears just where uncertainty intrudes on the cut-and-dried procedures of the plant—machinery breakdowns.

These breakdowns are frequent and unpredictable in this technology.[5] Every breakdown threatens the worker's achievement of his quota, interferes with the supervisor's scheduling of work and material, and touches the director's responsibility for the successful operation of the plant. Breakdowns are threatening to everyone in the plant except the technical engineer and his maintenance men, who have the de facto privilege of manipulating breakdowns to reward their friends and punish their enemies among the workers and supervisors. It is a maintenance man who inspects a breakdown, determines its seriousness, and decides what course of action to pursue. His performance is not subject to control or inspection by anyone but the technical engineer. Under these circumstances the permanent coalition between the technical engineer and the collectivity of maintenance men dominates several triads simultaneously. In the triad composed of the technical engineer, maintenance men, and production workers, it is a conservative coalition defending the superior status of the maintenance men in relation to the workers. In the triad composed of the technical engineer, maintenance men and foremen (or an individual foreman) the coalition between technical engineer and maintenance man is improper, for it undermines the foreman's authority and forces him into retreatism and ritualism in his supervisory role. In the triad composed of technical engineer, maintenance men, and assistant director, the coalition is revolutionary; it challenges the assistant director's right to give orders to the technical engineer and to manage the production process. In most of the plants observed by Crozier this revolutionary coalition prevailed. The technical engineer, backed by his loyal and competent crew of maintenance men, was able to make good his challenge to the assistant director's authority:

> The assistant director can give formal orders to the technical engineer but cannot control their execution. The technical engineer—who, of course, cannot give orders to his assistant director—can control his behavior, since he is able to set the limits of what is possible and what is not possible for him to do.[6]

[5] In order to protect the anonymity of the enterprise, Crozier describes the manufacturing process in vague terms, and the reader is not told enough about the machinery to judge whether the unpredictability of breakdowns is inherent in the technology or is artificially induced.

[6] Crozier, *op. cit.,* p. 125.

Curiously enough, this situation seems to place more stress on the technical engineer than on the assistant directors. An assistant director may be bitter, frustrated, or angry when he discovers the impossibility of exercising his legitimate authority, but his state of mind will not be desperate, for his inability to carry out the duties assigned to him has no serious consequences: it does not interfere with the routinized operation of the plant or with his own expectation of promotion or even with his relationship with the director, who is not ordinarily threatened by a power struggle between his subordinates and does not have either the power or the inclination to do anything about it.

The technical engineer, although successful in the triadic contests, is likely to feel the strain and to develop neurotic side-effects. Although he is almost certain to win his fight with an assistant director, there is no way for him to consolidate his gains since promotion to a higher rank is impossible. The defeat of the assistant director does not change the organization but merely isolates the technical engineer from the only other man in the plant with similar status and interests. Since assistant directors are rotated frequently, the technical engineer's victory is temporary. In the course of his long career in a single plant he will have to face and fight a long series of assistant directors, some better able to challenge him than others, without deriving much benefit from his past struggles.

Triads involving outsiders seem to be absent or unimportant in these plants. Although the technical engineer deals with outside contractors, the comptroller buys from outside suppliers, and the director is continually in touch with the Central Office, none of these relationships seem to take triadic form. In some other types of organization triads involving outsiders are much more conspicuous and important. These may be called *boundary triads*. From one point of view the sine qua non of an organization—its fundamental and essential characteristic—is that any two of its members interacting with an outsider in the performance of their organizational roles tend to form an automatic coalition of *we* against *you-and-your-associates*. We will now look at an organization whose operation cannot be understood without reference to boundary triads.

BOUNDARY TRIADS IN AN ADVERTISING AGENCY

W. Advertising, Inc., is a fairly typical "Madison Avenue" agency [7] located in Manhattan, although not on Madison Avenue. At the time

[7] Unpublished study by the author, 1961. For a description and sociological analysis of the advertising industry in English-speaking countries, see Jeremy Tunstall, *The Advertising Man in London Advertising Agencies* (London: Chapman & Hall, Ltd., 1964).

of the study it had about 600 employees, of whom thirty-two were vice-presidents, including four senior vice-presidents, two executive vice-presidents, and an executive vice-president and treasurer. The agency had twenty-three active clients, and for more than half of these it was the exclusive agency. However, three major clients accounted for more than 60 per cent of the total billings, and two of these major clients reserved some of their product lines for competitive agencies.

Our present concern is with the numerous vice-presidents and their relationships with clients. Most of the ordinary (or "buck") vice-presidents functioned as account executives. A few of them were responsible for specialized activities such as market research, graphic design, and a small foreign subsidiary. Each senior vice-president was nominally in charge of a group of related accounts but he actually spent most of his time on a single major account or, in one case, on a potential major account with the nominal account executive acting as his assistant. The executive vice-presidents had corporate responsibilities, met daily as an executive committee, and spent much of their time on financial and personnel problems.

The proliferation of vice-presidents is itself an interesting phenomenon. One way that agencies compete for clients is by offering to treat them as preferred clients and by assigning high-status personnel to work on their accounts. This competition leads to replacing the title of account executive—an earlier hyperbole—with the universally esteemed title of vice-president. The middle-ranking corporate officials who would normally be called personnel manager, director of research, or assistant comptroller in another industry, insist on equal designation and the class of vice-presidents expands still further. Considerable ingenuity is then required to find appropriate names for the higher officials who do exercise managerial functions. One agency has a Principal Executive Vice-President; another uses the title of Managing Director for a similar position.

The point of stress for every advertising agency is the maintenance of client relationships. The customs of the trade allow clients to withdraw all or part of their business from an agency and transfer it to a competing agency at any time without notice or discussion. Such changes are usually not announced in advance; an agency can seldom be certain of holding its major clients, even those on which its continued existence depends, for any set time. There are some exceptions, especially in "captive" agencies, those agencies which are owned by their clients, but these have quite different problems.

The agency's overriding concern in dealing with a client is not to jeopardize his goodwill. The client knows this and the agency is aware that he knows it. The client may therefore be as captious and demanding as he pleases. The agency must do its best to satisfy his demands, for any flagging of zeal will suggest to the client that he might obtain better service elsewhere.

Since an agency's ability to satisfy a client's demands is limited by its resources and by the demands of its other clients, and since the exigencies of the client are likely to grow more troublesome over time, major accounts are transferred from one agency to another fairly often. Agencies are constantly aware that the threat of transfer is real, and they remain on the alert for signs of client disaffection.

It will now be clear why the account executive is needed, why he is called a vice-president, and why he manages only a single account. The client insists on the instant attention of the agency when he telephones or visits or asks for a conference and he is allowed to make demands and create emergencies outside of business hours and at any place that suits his convenience. The agency people he works with must attach dramatic importance to minor fluctuations in the sales of his products.

Considerable attention is given to advertising in the day-by-day decisions of companies that sell consumer products. There is a continuous exchange of information between the company and the advertising agency about market conditions, competitors' activities, new product developments, the planning and scheduling of campaigns, and the outcome of promotional efforts. The client company usually designates one man to be responsible for liaison with the agency and he becomes the opposite number of the account executive.

The positions of client representatives in their own companies vary much more than those of account executives. Normally, they hold such titles as director of advertising or vice-president, marketing, but the client representatives with whom W. Advertising, Inc., dealt at the time of the study included a board chairman, several presidents, the son of a large stockholder, and two or three lowly product managers. Whatever the rank of the client representative, he is considered to be superior to the account executive when they interact. The relationship is likely to be uncomfortable when the client representative is a minor figure in his own organization and appears junior to the account executive. The client representative is called "the client" and is spoken of as if he alone embodied his company.

A coalition between the two men is obligatory, and if it is not formed the account executive will be replaced or the client will seek a new agency. They will talk to each other daily, meet several times a week, lunch together, and travel together. A steady flow of correspondence, data, and graphic material connects their offices and they keep few business secrets from each other, since their coalition rests upon a solid ground of common interest. If the campaigns they develop together are successful, each of them gains power and prestige in his own organization and in the eyes of competitors. Conversely, the failure of a campaign, especially if it appears to be a foolish failure, may be disastrous to them both.

To understand the place of this coalition in the several triads in which it plays a part we must examine the place of each partner in his own organization.

From the agency's standpoint, the role of the account executive poses a dilemma. If he does not succeed in establishing a close working partnership with the client, the latter is likely to look for a more congenial agency. But if the desired relationship is established, the client will become more attached to the account executive than to the agency he represents. When this happens, the account executive can consider the possibility of taking the client with him to another agency or even to a new agency of his own. Such actions fall within the normal expectations of the trade, although the agency that loses the account always feels outraged. The more successful an account executive is, the more valuable he becomes to his employer but the less reliable.

The structure of W. Advertising, Inc., is designed, more or less deliberately, to cope with this problem. The risk of defection is minimized by restricting every account executive to a single account and, if it is a major account, by assigning a senior vice-president to watch him. The assignments of each senior vice-president are carefully arranged so that he is never in contact with more than one major client at a time.

Competitiveness among account executives is encouraged by salary arrangements. In W. Advertising, Inc., for example, no two account executives receive the same salary. The differences are not explicable by age, experience, service with the agency, or any other rational criterion. Account executives are prohibited from helping one another, ostensibly to protect the secrets of clients. The agency fosters competition between account executives for agency resources, and conflicting requests are met in a deliberately arbitrary and enigmatic way. Little love is lost among the account executives and there is not much danger of group defection.

The relationships between the account executive and the department heads, on whom he must call for such services as graphic design, production, and market research, are also strained. The account executive needs their active cooperation but has no power to command it. He is pressured by his client to seek priorities and special services which the service departments have no motive to provide. The account executive's total responsibility for his account averts blame from the service department when it blunders.

The situation of the client representative is less predictable. In some companies he is a top executive or an owner and is therefore not subject to much pressure from above. Usually, however, his situation parallels that of the account executive. As a product manager he must compete with other product managers for limited resources and arbitrary rewards, and he will probably discover that the product development and manufacturing divisions are unable or unwilling to provide the resources he requires to meet the sales goals imposed on him by the corporate management.

In the situation we have been describing, the usual expectation—that in a boundary triad the two actors from the same organization will form a coalition—is reversed. The account executive and the client representative participate together in a number of boundary triads and generally choose each other over their fellow-employees. To illustrate, let us review the boundary triads in which one account executive and his matching client representative of one major account were involved at the time of the study.

A number of these triads involved subordinates of either man who worked in close touch with both of them. In these triads, the coalition was conservative and dominant. The third parties in other significant triads included the chairman of the board of the client company, the president of the agency, the president of the client company, and the senior vice-president to whom the account executive reported. In the latter two triads, the coalition was openly rebellious. In the triads involving the heads of each organization the coalition was conservative but very solidary.

There were no active triads that included a peer of either partner. The account executive carefully avoided the one other vice-president of the client company, although this forced him to obtain some essential information through indirect channels. The client representative was habitually rude to other account executives in the agency.

The inability of the agency to meet the client's demands provoked antagonism between the two organizations. The client company demanded a more favorable position among the agency's clients than its volume of business warranted and a higher level of performance in promoting its products than the agency considered possible. In these respects it was a fairly typical client: it continually threatened the agency with termination of its account.

The coalition of the account executive and the client representative became a kind of shock absorber, absorbing and dissipating the tension between the two organizations. From the standpoint of the client representative, the agency was divided into a faction of friends headed by the account executive and a faction of antagonists that included most of the agency's top management. The friends offered the limitless help and cooperation a client wants from an agency, while the antagonists seemed to be uncooperative, uninformed, and careless of the client's interests.

The agency's inability to meet the client's expectations was not looked upon as the account executive's fault, but rather as a problem that he and the client representative faced jointly.

From the viewpoint of the account executive, the client company was similarly bifurcated. His friends, headed by the client representative, were reasonable men who were fully aware of what advertising could and could not accomplish. The rest of the company's management he regarded as overbearing, unreasonable, and unappreciative. He looked to his friend, the client representative, to protect him against their caprices.

The persons that each partner avoided in the other's organization—the potential peers of the other partner—appeared to them in an even worse light. In the conversation of the coalition they were described only half-facetiously as criminals and mental defectives. Relationships were held to such a minimal level that, if the account executive had been removed, the client representative would have been unable and unwilling to select a substitute for him. In the client company the client representative's only peer was the vice-president in charge of production, whom the account executive managed never to meet at all.

It was evident even to the partners themselves that each of them could create problems for the other and they occasionally did so under the guise of relaying information. For example, when the client representative informed the account executive that the president of the client company had set an impossible deadline for the completion of a project, the account executive had no way of knowing whether his partner had argued passionately for an extension of time, as he claimed; had accepted the deadline without argument; or had, in fact, proposed it himself. Similarly, when the account executive announced that the deadline could not be met because his request for additional personnel had been turned down by his senior vice-president, the client representative had no way of ascertaining how forcefully the request had been made, or whether it had been made at all.

These stratagems, practiced in moderation, reinforced the mutual respect of the two partners and preserved the pleasant tone of their relationship. Their coalition, like most coalitions, did not imply either a boundless friendship or an unlimited partnership. It did guarantee that each of them would treat the other as well as their opposing interests dictated, and perhaps somewhat better. To achieve this balance in the boundary situation, each partner sacrificed some of his interests within his own organization. Since a faint aura of disloyalty colors any coalition across an organizational boundary, the antagonism that develops between each man and his superiors will in all probability have some damaging effect on the future career of each. Within the advertising agency, in which relationships like this were common and their usefulness was recognized, there was a tendency to overlook the antagonisms developed in a boundary triad. Sociological insight was not so well developed in the client company. The president could not bring himself to forgive the client representative's alliance with an outsider, and after some time he was able to arrange for his dismissal. However, there was close cooperation between the two organizations as long as the triad persisted.

Any sustained liaison between organizations will create a set of boundary triads that function continuously.[8] Boundary triads will also develop between two organizations in conflict, but they will be terminal in character and typically short-lived.

A CASE OF ORGANIZATIONAL CONFLICT

In a protracted conflict the formation of coalitions often changes the character and identity of the parties so that a succession of new triads emerges from the ruins of those destroyed by terminal coalitions. Sometimes, as in the case to be described, the underlying issue remains unchanged while the opposing positions are upheld by a series of protagonists.

The basic paradigm of conflict is a triad composed of two antagonists and a witness, whose support is solicited by both antagonists. This support, if granted, may vary in form from tacit approval to a full coalition between the witness and one of the antagonists. When the latter occurs, that particular phase of the contest is resolved, although the issues that caused it may not be settled. New antagonists accompanied by new witnesses may emerge to continue the conflict.

ANALYSIS OF A CIVIC CONTROVERSY

Meyerson and Banfield [9] describe a controversy over low-rent public housing in Chicago, after the passage of the Federal Housing and Redevelopment Act by Congress in 1949 authorized the construction of 40,000 units of low-rent public housing in that city. The disputed question was whether the projects should be located on vacant land in outlying districts or on land obtained by clearing slums. If projects were built on vacant land, they would not contribute to urban improvement; if on occupied land, they would make little or no addition to the total supply of rental housing.

8 The continuous, episodic, and terminal situations are described in Chap. 1 of this volume.

9 Martin Meyerson and Edward C. Banfield, *Politics, Planning, and the Public Interest: The Case of Public Housing in Chicago* (New York: Free Press of Glencoe, Inc., 1955).

Beneath this manifest issue lay the question of segregation. It was expected by both sides that the population to be housed would include a considerable proportion of Negroes. This expectation was sufficient to guarantee opposition to the projects in residential neighborhoods. Even mixed or predominantly Negro neighborhoods opposed the projects on the grounds that they would lower property values or alter a satisfactory racial balance.

If all of the projects were built in slum areas, where neighborhood opposition was not a serious obstacle, thousands of dwellings would have to be demolished before any new units were available to relocate the displaced families. Moreover, the high cost of occupied land would require slum clearance projects to have a high density of occupants, which would increase the overcrowding of public facilities in those districts.

The parties initially involved were the Housing Authority, the City Council, and the Mayor. The Authority was an independent public body composed of five commissioners who were appointed but could not be removed by the Mayor. Its chairman was a Negro businessman and its executive head was a nationally known housing expert whose views were more liberal than those of the commissioners. The City Council was composed of fifty aldermen, each representing a ward. The Democrats had a solid majority based on an old-fashioned party machine. An inner circle of Democratic aldermen controlled the Council. This circle, like the machine, was dominated by Irish Catholics.

The previous mayor had been the undisputed political boss of Chicago and Cook County and had run the City Council autocratically. The new Mayor, who had been elected as a reform candidate and who had had little previous experience in politics, was pledged to respect the Council's independence.

Before the outbreak of the controversy, the Authority enjoyed a friendly but distant relationship with the municipal government. The housing projects built in the earlier period had been financed jointly by the city and state. The new program was to be financed by the federal government; but a special act of the state legislature authorized the City Council to approve or disapprove project sites. The first sign of an impending conflict appeared in October 1949, when the chairman of the Authority called on the Mayor and presented the Authority's proposal to build about 10,000 units of low-rent housing on seven sites.

"Go talk it over with Duffy," the Mayor told him as Taylor later recalled. "Work it out with Duffy—it's the alderman's affair."

"No," said Taylor, "the commissioners think the matter ought to be discussed and decided upon in public. We have decided to present the program to the Council publicly."

"I differ," the Mayor said, "but if that's the way you want it, go ahead."

"We want you to look over our selections and give us your personal opinion," Taylor remembered saying to the Mayor. "Then we would like to have you present the sites to the Council with your endorsement."

"Give me a week to think it over," the Mayor replied.[10]

When the chairman returned three weeks later, the papers were still unread. The Mayor explained that the aldermen would be resentful if he took any position regarding the sites before they learned of them. He had therefore taken care not to learn anything about the sites—even from newspaper stories.

This was the Authority's first effort to form a coalition with the Mayor against the Council. The Authority overestimated the political strength of its supporters throughout the controversy and believed it was backed by overwhelming popular pressure, which the Mayor could not disregard. It may also have overestimated the Mayor's interest in the Authority, whose commissioners he appointed.

The details of the site proposals were soon published, having been quietly released by Authority staff members who feared that discussions with the Mayor might lead to a compromise. To forestall this possibility and make it impossible for the chairman of the Authority to bargain with either the Mayor or the Council, these staff members arranged for publicity in the *Sun-Times,* a newspaper with an editorial policy that favored low-rent public housing. The aldermen were annoyed by this action, which was intended to hinder negotiation about the political consequences of the site proposals. When a proposal was formally submitted to the Council, public hearings were held but action was delayed indefinitely.

At this time the Authority called upon its outside supporters; twenty-five delegates of housing organizations spoke to the Mayor, but he refused to use his influence with the Council, insisting that the aldermen had a duty to decide for themselves. Another delegation spoke to the political boss who had selected the Mayor for nomination, but failed to persuade him to intervene in the matter. The leader of the aldermen's opposition to the site proposals was also approached unsuccessfully.

At the same time, the Authority sought support through the newspapers. On several occasions the Mayor objected to this publicity and asked the Authority not to embarrass him in his dealings with the press. The officials responsible for the stories looked upon the Mayor's protests as evidence that the pressure was becoming effective.

An attempt was made to recruit mass support for the site proposals through the Public Housing Association, liberal labor unions, and religious groups. As these organizations proposed plans for "mass action" the opposition, which included citywide organizations such as the Real

10 *Ibid.,* p. 171.

Estate Board and neighborhood associations such as the Southwest Neighborhood Council, packed the galleries at the Council's public hearings with angry housewives who hooted and screamed whenever an advocate of public housing took the floor. The Mayor appeared only when antihousing testimony was being heard. After the hearings, the housing committee of the Council recommended two of the seven proposed sites, but it refused either to approve or reject the others. The Mayor then announced that if conflict developed between the Authority and the Council, he would side with the Council because its members represented the people. However, he did urge the Council to approve a large-scale plan for public housing and tried to persuade the Council leaders to meet privately with the key people in the Authority. When the Authority's supporters in the Public Housing Association learned of the Mayor's position, they wrote him an open letter requesting permission for an observer of their own to be present at any negotiations over which the Mayor might preside.

A subcommittee of the Council then chartered a bus and visited a large number of possible sites. The members of the subcommittee were overwhelmingly opposed to public housing and so they systematically searched for sites that would embarrass the proponents of the program. Their recommendations were deplored even in the conservative press and the Authority's position seemed to be strengthened.

The Mayor then announced that he had invited the leading aldermen and commissioners of the Authority to a meeting in his office. He told the press in advance that these gentlemen would be compelled to work together until they came up with an acceptable public housing program and that he would remain with them until the problem was solved. Again, the officials of the Authority acted to avert a possible compromise. They persuaded the commissioners to prepare new site proposals and to make them public just before the meeting arranged by the Mayor at his office. At the meeting, the aldermen blamed the Authority for the Council's refusal to adopt a housing program. After the meeting broke up, the Mayor scolded the commissioners for their uncooperativeness.

Several days later the Authority's new proposals were considered by the Council. However, the Mayor asked the Council not to act on the proposals and instead suggested that another committee be appointed to negotiate with the Authority. The Mayor's ostensible reason for delaying action was his apprehension that a negative vote might end all consideration of public housing for the time being, but some of the aldermen opposed to public housing said later that they had been prepared to accept the new site proposals until the Mayor suggested a delay. Others believed that the Mayor's intervention gave the antihousing faction their first inkling that the program might be defeated completely.

A self-appointed, unofficial committee of influential aldermen began to prepare a compromise plan of their own that had different goals than the Authority's. These aldermen wanted a minimum amount of public housing, enough to provide for destitute, eligible families but not enough to attract migrants, especially Negro migrants, to the city. Their criteria for site selection were essentially negative. They proposed that projects not be located on vacant land suitable for private development, or in proximity to middle-class neighborhoods, or in the wards of friendly aldermen. Their suggested compromise eventually included eight slum sites, all in Negro districts, and seven sites on vacant land, mostly in the wards of aldermen who had supported public housing and were in this way to be punished for it. According to their proposal very few units would be built on vacant land and the number of families to be displaced by the entire program would be approximately equal to the number rehoused; so that the net addition to the housing supply would be negligible.

The Mayor and the leading aldermen, acting now as a coalition, summoned the commissioners to a secret meeting in a hotel room and urged them to accept the compromise plan. Public opinion seemed to favor it. Most of the Authority's supporters had not been able to follow the details of the long series of proposals and counterproposals. The compromise plan seemed to satisfy the minimum requirements and assure that the opportunity to use Federal funds for residential construction would not be lost. Even the *Sun-Times,* heretofore the Authority's voice, urged acceptance, as did the Plan Commission and other city agencies.

The compromise plan was wholly unsatisfactory to the Authority and its staff with regard to density, relocation, land classification, and other detailed provisions. Since the funds for the program would be provided by a Federal agency, the Public Housing Administration, and that agency was opposed to segregation or inequitable treatment of the races, the Authority hoped that the aldermen's compromise, with its obvious anti-Negro bias, would be rejected in Washington. The head of the Authority went to Washington to explain this situation and received a sympathetic reception until a representative of the Mayor appeared on the scene and reported that no other plan was likely to be politically acceptable in Chicago. To the surprise and distress of the Authority's officials, the Federal agency supported the Mayor and stated that they would approve the compromise plan with certain nominal changes.

By this time the matter was virtually settled, although discussion continued. The Mayor's representative prepared an elaborate report at the Authority's expense explaining how the compromise plan could be implemented in stages without creating a relocation problem even as the staff of the Authority urged the reluctant commissioners to reject it. The *Sun-Times* changed its editorial policy and ceased to feature stories on public housing. The chairman of the Authority made further attempts to obtain the intervention of the White House and of the Democratic National Committee, but when these failed, the compromise plan was accepted by the commissioners. It had still to be approved by the Council and to overcome a last-minute spurt of opposition from aldermen *favoring* public housing, but eventually it passed by a large majority and the controversy was over.

In subsequent months two of the vacant sites and the only white slum site in the compromise package were eliminated for various reasons. Belated opposition developed among the race-relations advisors of the Public Housing Administration who came to regard the Chicago program as discriminatory, and it was more than a year before final approval was obtained from Washington. By that time, the personnel and character of the Authority had completely changed: the staff were now construction-minded, and as the political issues receded into the past, demolition proceeded with little attention to relocation. The projects as ultimately constructed reinforced the existing pattern of racial segregation.

In many ways this was a typical public controversy, centered around a fundamental difference of interest: on the one hand, a national movement to improve the housing of poor (and incidentally Negro) families in urban slums; on the other, the desire of the aldermen and their constituents to preserve neighborhood barriers based on income and color. Individuals and organizations changed sides from time to time, but the basic roles of proponent, opponent, and witness were enacted throughout the struggle.

In this instance, the witness was personified with unusual clarity by the Mayor. The Authority detected his leaning towards the opposition very early and, overestimating its own popular support, it devoted more effort to finding a substitute witness than to wooing the Mayor. But each individual or party invited to assume the role of witness—the President, the political bosses, the Democratic National Committee, the Plan Commission, the Public Housing Administration—sniffed the political atmosphere and came to the same conclusion as the Mayor.

When the original site proposals failed to attract adequate support, the public housing program was not abandoned, but its purposes were transformed. It became a program to provide improved housing for a limited number of low-income families without threatening established patterns of segregation. This modification was accomplished by a coalition of the Council majority and the Mayor.

The Mayor, like the other participants, was moved by the forces of the situation, but he enjoyed enough freedom of action to tip the balance, or seem to do so, at the turning points of the conflict.

X

THE MARCH
OF HISTORY

We turn now to triads whose actors are much larger collectivities: political parties, social classes, nations, and even groups of nations. History is largely a chronicle of organized conflict and its results, and organized conflict is a triadic phenomenon.

THE CONFLICT TRIAD

In the previous chapter we examined briefly the role of the witness in a small-scale conflict between collectivities. The term *witness* may be misleading in connection with conflicts of larger scale, but alternate terms like *mediator* and *neutral* carry connotations of impartiality that are appropriate in some conflicts but not in all.[1]

Serious conflict is necessarily two-sided and it is important to understand why this is so. The only conflicts that lack a witness are those that divide the social universe into two inclusive parties,

[1] For a formal model of the triad in which the witness *is* a neutral mediator, see Joseph E. McGrath, "A Social Psychological Approach to the Study of Negotiation," in Raymond V. Bowers, ed., *Studies on Behavior in Organizations: A Research Symposium* (Athens, Ga.: University of Georgia Press, 1966), pp. 101–34. The role of witnesses in resolving interdepartmental conflict in industry is examined in Richard E. Walton, *Third Party Roles in Interdepartmental Conflict,* Purdue University, Institute for Research in the Behavioral, Economic and Management Sciences, Paper #184, 1967.

for example a world war without any neutral states or an unobserved war between two completely isolated tribes. In all other cases, the social field of a conflict, from the standpoint of a protagonist, is divided into three parts—his own side, the other side, and a group of potential intervenors. A protagonist's own side may, of course, also be divided into factions, but its action against the enemy must be unified if it is to have any chance of success. In a battle or any other form of decisive encounter some disaffected factions may not participate while others desert to the enemy. These realignments are part of the process of polarization, and they accentuate the two-sidedness of the conflict.

A party to a conflict may even face multiple opponents who have no communication with each other. Nevertheless, he knows that if these opponents meet at the same time and place they will almost certainly act in concert. Even if they refused to communicate or insisted on acting separately, they would constitute a single party in the tactical calculations of the other side. Many a battlefield has been approached by three or four armies of uncertain inclination, but every battle is ultimately fought and decided by only two armies.[2]

There may also be multiple witnesses of a conflict, each witness forming a distinct triad with the two antagonists and thus there may be a considerable number of these triads at the scene of a particular conflict. The witness to an organized conflict is both an observer and a potential intervenor. We would not classify as witnesses those observers who are so detached from the situation or so weak in relation to the antagonists that they cannot influence the outcome. The witness may intervene by interrupting the conflict or by forming a coalition with one of the antagonists. If he puts a stop to the conflict, he may have protected the probable loser. If he forms a coalition, his intention is to decide the conflict in favor of his partner. Even if he decides to abstain, the witness may determine the outcome of the conflict either because he allows the stronger contestant to proceed to victory without interference, or because his abstention causes a sudden loss of strength for the side on whose behalf he was expected to intervene.

As noted before, there is nothing that compels all of the witnesses of a particular conflict to unite with one of the antagonists, but the furor created by a conflict in a social system draws witnesses, and if the struggle lasts long enough, more and more of them will be drawn in until most

[2] Although the alliances on either side may be temporary. According to Clausewitz, "Even if two states really go to war with a third, they do not always both look in like measure upon this common enemy as one that they must destroy or be destroyed themselves. The affair is often settled like a commercial transaction; each, according to the amount of the risk he incurs or the advantage to be expected, takes a share in the concern . . ."—Karl von Clausewitz, *War, Politics and Power,* trans. E. M. Collins (Chicago: Henry Regnery Co., 1962), p. 251.

members of the system are involved. The witness who joins a conflict by forming a coalition with one of the antagonists almost always hopes and expects that the new coalition will dominate the triad, but the outcome of any conflict is inherently uncertain and there is always a possibility that the intervention will fail, either because the strength of the parties has been miscalculated or because a new witness, attracted by the con- flict in its modified form, intervenes in turn.

WAR AND PEACE

World War I, for example, began with a quarrel between Austria and Serbia over the assassination of the Austrian heir to the Austro-Hungarian throne, Archduke Francis Ferdinand, who was killed on a visit to Serbia. Austria issued a harsh ultimatum to Serbia. Germany immediately of- fered unqualified support to Austria. Great Britain tried unsuccessfully to prevent the conflict. Russia mobilized on behalf of Serbia. France, allied to Russia, refused to stand aside, whereupon Germany declared war upon France and demanded that Belgium allow free passage to German troops. The Belgians refused, joining the Allies; Great Britain intervened in turn, and the initial phase of the war was on. A few months later, Turkey joined the Central Powers, and Bulgaria did so the fol- lowing year. Italy, having abandoned her alliance with Germany and Austria at the outbreak of the war, entered on the side of the Allies in 1915, followed by Roumania in 1916, and Greece in 1917. The American decision to join the Allies in 1917 completed the process of polarization, and—with the possible exception of Sweden—exhausted the supply of powerful witnesses.

All this is fairly obvious. Indeed, after the exhaustive research that has been conducted on the origins of recent wars, there is not much mys- tery about how they begin and why some of them enlarge. Throughout the twentieth century it has been almost as plain to the man in the street as to the men in the chancellories that any minor international crisis attracts powerful witnesses and polarizes enormous forces on the brink of war.

Given a social system that contains a number of potentially hostile collectivities in close contact with each other, there appear to be only two possible outcomes aside from war—imperial domination or a balance of power. Of these two forms of peace, imperial domination is probably the more stable, judging from the experience of the Mongols from the time of Genghis Khan to Timur and from that of the Romans from Hadrian to Constantine. The imperial power must be cohesive and its regular forces must be much stronger than any possible combination of oppo- nents. These conditions have not prevailed in the West since the death of Constantine: the empires of Charlemagne, Charles V, Napoleon, and

Hitler fell apart almost as soon as they were founded. The demographic and cultural composition of Europe suggests why. An imperial power that is cohesive and indivisible cannot include more than a small minority of the total population. Since the culturally separate nations of the Western world stand fairly close to each other with respect to scientific and social development, it has not so far been possible for any potential imperial power to overcome its numerical disadvantage by means of military or administrative superiority alone. The failures of Napoleon and Hitler to establish imperial domination by military conquest are instructive. The inability of the United States to maintain its brief monopoly of atomic weapons illustrates the difficulty of consolidating a technological advantage over technologically advanced competitors.

The colonial empires of the European powers were originally established by minuscule forces whose sailing ships and firearms gave them an overwhelming military advantage.[3] During the four centuries of colonialism ships became bigger, faster, and less dependent on the elements, the power and portability of firearms increased, and a worldwide network of mails and eventually wires provided superior communications. Nevertheless, the disparity of numbers between rulers and natives made colonial rule uneasy everywhere except in North America and Australia, where Europeans displaced the native inhabitants to become the majority. In the other continents, the military advantage of European rulers was eroded by the diffusion of technology—especially at the end of the colonial era when radio provided a low-cost communication network for every resistance group, and air travel put rebel leaders within easy reach of potential allies. It took hardly more than a decade after World War II for most of the territories under European control to gain their independence.

BALANCES OF POWER

When circumstances do not permit either the establishment of an imperium or the merger of contending powers into a unified superstate, the only form of peace attainable is a balance of power. The condition is familiar and its instability is notorious.[4] For our present purposes a

---

[3] Admirably documented by Carlo M. Cipolla, *Guns and Sails in the Early Phase of European Expansion: 1400–1700* (London: William Collins, Sons & Co., Ltd., 1965).

[4] See, among other recent discussions of international balances of power, Quincy Wright, *A Study of War* (2nd ed.) (Chicago: University of Chicago Press, 1965); George Liska, *International Equilibrium* (Cambridge, Mass.: Harvard University Press, 1967); William H. Riker, *The Theory of Political Coalitions* (New Haven and London: Yale University Press, 1962); Morton A. Kaplan, *System and Process in International Politics* (New York: John Wiley & Sons, Inc., 1957); and "Balance of Power, Bipolarity and Other Models of International Systems," *American Political Science Review*, LI (1967), 684–95; and Morton A. Kaplan, Arthur Burns, and Richard Quandt, "Theoretical Analysis of 'Balance of Power,'" *Behavioral Science*, V (1960), 240–52.

balance of power will be defined as a stable power distribution in a triad without coalitions.[5] The definition implies the theory.

The situation includes three or more organized collectivities contending for advantage in the same area, not subject to a common sovereign, and capable of making war. Over some appreciable interval of time peace prevails and no coalition is formed. This is a balance of power.

Taking the powers three at a time, we observe that they have contending interests, are not restrained by a superior authority, are armed and capable of war, but remain at peace for an appreciable interval. None of the three possible coalitions forms. It may be inferred from these facts that the strongest power is not stronger than the other two combined. Nor is the strongest power just equal to the two others combined; for in that case the others would be virtually forced into a coalition. The balance of power triad must be assumed to be one of those types in which any coalition is a winning coalition.[6]

If such a coalition were formed, went to war, and won as expected, the triad would be reduced, at least temporarily, to the dyad of the winners. They would still be independent powers with incompatible interests, but the weaker would now be completely at the mercy of the stronger, supposing their gains in the late war to be either approximately equal or proportionate to their resources. The prospect of eventual subjugation ought to deter any power from entering into a coalition with a stronger partner in the first place.

The Type 5 triad, which has no equal members and thus allows for no coalition between equals, is the simplest form of the balance of power. In triads of Types 1, 2 and 3 coalitions between equals are possible and the foregoing constraint does not apply to all possible coalitions. However, other constraints on the formation of coalitions may be equally effective.

A potential partner may be anathema on political or religious grounds, even though the tactical advantages of the coalition are obvious. Conservative regimes do not readily embrace revolutionary leaders; Hindus and Moslems are slow to seize an opportunity to combine forces. Exceptions immediately spring to mind; but there can be no serious question that ideological differences prevent many advantageous coalitions.

The analysis of tactical situations in the real world cannot begin with the assumption that gains and losses are equally weighted. Not every actor's desire for a gain equals his desire to avoid a comparable loss nor is a gain about as desirable as a comparable loss inflicted on an opponent.

[5] Kaplan, in the works just cited, sets a minimum of five members for a working balance of power, which may explain the rigidity and complexity of the policy rules which nations must follow, according to Kaplan, to maintain a balance of power.

[6] See Chap. 1 in this volume.

Most collectivities are conservative with respect to their goals; they are more eager to avoid losses than to make comparable gains. Only a few aggressive powers follow a consistent policy of weighting potential gains as heavily as potential losses in their tactical calculations.

The weighting of gains and losses against a partner's gains and losses is still more intricate. Even in very simple situations, like laboratory games, it cannot be assumed that an actor belonging to a coalition is interested only in his own gains and losses and is indifferent to those of his partner, for a partner is often more feared than an opponent, and a player may forego a gain for himself to prevent a similar gain by his partner.

Another reason why a winning coalition does not always appear when there is an opportunity is that when a coalition involves a merger of forces, the leaders of one or both factions will lose some of their autonomy.

But a balance of power is not created by the mere reluctance of the powers in a triad to form coalitions. Indeed, if it were known with certainty that no coalition would be formed under any circumstances, there would be no balance; any stronger power would be free to attack a weaker neighbor. The essential feature of the situation is that although no coalitions have formed, the possibility of a coalition remains, and the likelihood of a coalition will increase sharply if the existing power distribution is disturbed. When one power in such a triad attacks another, it is immediately evident to the third power that the attack, if successful, will lead to a merger of the contending powers or force the vanquished power into a coalition with the victor and that the new power or coalition will be able to dominate him. Whatever the circumstances that formerly prevented coalitions, the third power now would have compelling reasons to join the weaker party to the conflict. Thus each power in the triad is restrained from attacking another by the expectation that his attack would provoke the other two powers into a winning coalition against him.

The weakness of the balance of power as an engine of social control is that a power facing two roughly equal powers can never be sure that they will not revise their calculations and eventually form a coalition. If such an event seems to be imminent, he may choose the lesser of two evils by initiating a coalition himself, even if it must be a dangerous alliance with a stronger partner. The 1939 war, it will be remembered, was launched by the announcement of an alliance between Hitler and Stalin that dissolved the European balance of power and freed Germany to attack its neighbors. That coalition was formed between two regimes whose ideological differences were as bitter and as irreconcilable as any in modern times, and it involved enormous risks for the weaker partner,

the Soviet Union, as later events showed. The threat of a coalition between the Nazis and the British-French alliance seems implausible now,
but it was plausible to Stalin in 1939, and even now it seems no more
unlikely than the coalition that actually was formed.[7]

A balance of power may be tipped in several other ways. Even simple
miscalculation will do it, for since each power in such a triad is probably
willing to enter a coalition with a weaker partner at any time, if the
weaker power miscalculates and supposes itself to be stronger, such an
offer may be cheerfully accepted.

The triad may become unbalanced because of internal developments.
One party may increase in strength or another decline until the triad is
imperceptibly transformed and the necessary condition for a balance of
power—that any two of the parties can form a winning coalition—is no
longer satisfied.

But the major source of instability in situations in which peace is
maintained by a balance of power is the linkage of balanced and unbalanced triads. Unless the three parties in a balance of power encom-
pass the world, each of them and each pair of them will be simultaneously involved in unbalanced triads in which there are active coalitions.
Events that occur in these other triads may be impossible to contain
within the delicate structure of the balanced triad. In 1914, the balance
of power among Germany, France, and Russia was destroyed in a few
days by Serbia's refusal to submit to the domination of Germany and
Austria.

Another unsettling effect of linkage is that the relative strength of
balanced powers may become indeterminable. This is likely to happen
when they have coalition partners in other triads who may or may not
support them in a war-like confrontation. In the 1914 war it was not
clear until the last moment that France would support Russia, that
Great Britain would support France, that Belgium would resist Germany, or that Italy would refuse to be bound by the Triple Alliance. In
both of the great wars it could not be determined for many months
after the outbreak whether the United States would join Britain and
France. In crucial modern cases, these uncertainties have led most of the
powers to overestimate their chances of success when deciding to engage
in active hostilities and to underestimate the costs of either victory or
defeat.

These examples on a grand scale should not conceal the fact that simi-

---

[7] By secret negotiation while the Russians simultaneously engaged in open negotiations with the French and British on a mutual-assistance treaty against German attack,
and the Germans sent a secret emissary to London. See Fred Charles Iklé, *How Nations
Negotiate* (New York: Harper & Row, Publishers, 1964), Chap. 4.

lar processes are at work in the relationship of smaller conflict groups such as political parties.

THE PARLIAMENTARY TRIAD

Parliamentary bodies divide themselves more or less spontaneously into Right, Left, and Center blocs. In somewhat oversimplified terms, the Center is attached to the status quo or, more precisely, to the continuation of current trends; the Right wants to return to the real or fancied conditions of the past; and the Left is committed to change. When a polity is relatively unified, the moderates in the Center are flanked by conservatives on the Right and liberals on the Left. When the constitutional order is not universally accepted, the Right Wing is better described as reactionary and the Left Wing as radical, each plotting to overthrow the parliamentary structure and establish its own regime.

The content of political ideologies varies a good deal between, say, Guatemala and Greece or, for that matter, between the United States and Great Britain,[8] but all such configurations have features in common. The Right represents hereditary advantage, the privileges of property, the status order of the previous generation, the political ambitions of the army, and the secular interests of the Church. Its active supporters are people who enjoy or claim privileges that seem to them to be vanishing. The Left, in modern politics, is always socialist to some degree, although the differences between the revolutionary temper of a communist deputy in France or Italy and the diluted collectivism of a liberal Democrat in the United States are more striking than their resemblances. Parties of the Left are always conceived of as mass parties even when their actual constituencies are very small. They represent the people who lack personal power and who must rely on their numbers and their solidarity to counteract the superior resources of their opponents. The Left prefers the future to the past and regards social change as essentially beneficial. Its greatest source of strength is the belief that history is on its side, that whether the political goals of the Left are hastened or delayed they are certain to be achieved in the long run.

The triadic configuration of Right, Left, and Center does not imply the existence of three parties. The number of political parties in a parliamentary system seems to be determined by the electoral machinery together with certain features of the national society. Simple majority voting favors a two-party system. Proportional representation stimulates

---

[8] For a detailed discussion of the type of differences that are relevant to coalition behavior, see the comparison of British and American politics in S. M. Lipset, *The First New Nation* (New York: Basic Books, Inc., 1963).

the growth of multiple small parties. Sequential voting seems to lead to the organization of temporary parties for particular occasions.[9] Regional parties usually develop whenever regions are sufficiently differentiated to seek autonomy. Anticonstitutional parties are certain to arise on the extreme right in recently established parliamentary systems and on the extreme left wherever the missionary activities of the Soviet Union and the Chinese People's Republic have not been successfully repressed.

Three-party systems are rather rare. According to Duverger [10] there have been only a few important examples of a three-party system in modern times: in Australia when an agrarian party was added to the Conservative-Labour dualism, and for a brief period about 1900, when Socialist parties emerged in England, Belgium, Sweden, and several other countries having two-party systems.

The usual alternatives are a two-party system, as in the United States and Great Britain, or a multiparty system, as in France, Italy, and West Germany. In a two-party system both parties are parties of the Center with their own right and left wings. One party—the Republicans or the Tories—lies further to the right, but the overlap is so considerable that most members of a party could transfer to the other party without changing places on the political spectrum. In such a system party discipline is necessarily poor. Except for a few crucial issues that involve the survival of a majority, legislators are free to take either side of any question. The great majority of voters are not dues-paying party members; even those who are regular members generally feel quite free to vote for candidates of the other party. Within each party there are distinguishable blocs, like the southern Democrats in the Senate or the trade-unionists in the House of Commons, whose positions on many questions are closer to the majority opinion in the other party than to that in their own. Such groups are likely to be especially active in the maneuvering and negotiation that accompanies the formation of legislative majorities on critical issues.

Multiparty systems usually include several major parties and a fringe of minor and incipient parties which can be arrayed on a more or less continuous scale of opinion from left to right. It is the practice in most multiparty legislatures to seat the deputies according to their position on this scale, with communists at the extreme left and monarchists or fascists at the extreme right.

The solidarity of parties varies greatly. It tends to be greater at the extremes of the array, but there are numerous exceptions. Some parties

[9] For a detailed exposition of the relationship between electoral machinery and the party system, see Maurice Duverger, *Political Parties* (2nd ed.) (London: Methuen & Co., Ltd., 1961).

[10] *Ibid.*, p. 234–36.

of the Center splinter into factions when excluded from the ruling coalition, but others are fairly cohesive.

Not only can the parties in a multiparty system be arranged on a continuum from right to left, they can also be grouped into three distinct categories as parties of the Left, the Center, and the Right, and these designations are generally unequivocal even when a right-wing party calls itself "Radical Socialists" or a left-wing party calls itself "Independent Republicans." Just as subparties develop in a two-party system, superparties often appear in a multiparty system when the parties of the Left join together in a popular front or the parties of the Right combine in a nationalist movement or a group of Center parties form a semipermanent alliance.

The coalition process is at the heart of any parliamentary system of government, since a winning coalition must be assembled in order for any legislative action to be taken. In the process of forming the coalition, bargains are struck that modify the proposed legislation, sometimes out of all recognition. A governing party with a considerable majority will have less trouble assembling winning coalitions than one with a bare majority or one with a majority in opposition to the government,[11] but this will not relieve it of the necessity of assembling a coalition. On controversial issues, the majority party is certain to find some of its members in opposition, and to carry such a vote, it must obtain support from members of the other party. These shifts are by no means random ones. A proposition with a leftward inclination will lose support in the right wing of the majority party and gain it from the left wing of the minority party. After repeated episodes of coalition formation, the position of most members on most issues will become predictable, and the effort to assemble a majority will be concentrated on a few individuals who are still uncommitted. In the nature of the case, the men whose minds are not made up are a little more likely to be found near the center of the political spectrum than at the extremes. Thus two-party systems seem to magnify the influence of moderates, and, in recent American and British experience, there has been a tendency for the overlap of opinion to increase to the point where there is practically no difference between the central positions of the two parties. Fundamental differences in two-party systems are expressed by the reorganization of the old pair of parties into a new pair. But this occurs with majestic slowness. The transformation of major parties has occurred about every two generations in the United States and at even longer intervals in Britain.

In a typical multiparty system the coalition process is directed towards

[11] A common situation in presidential systems like the American, but impossible in cabinet systems like the British.

the formation of a majority or large plurality that is capable of organizing a cabinet and a government. Except under unusual circumstances, no party can do this by itself and thus coalitions are a constitutional necessity in states with multiparty systems. The members of the new cabinet, who become the executives of the new government, are drawn from the several parties in the coalition. The number and importance of the portfolios given to each party is proportioned to the amount of support it contributes to the coalition, with some adjustment for the talents of individual leaders. Governing coalitions are usually formed by adjacent parties on the political spectrum. In a stable parliamentary system a governing coalition will normally represent an alliance of Center parties with adjacent parties of the Left or of the Right, but not of both. Such a government falls when it moves further to the right or left than its components on the other margin are willing to tolerate. When the Center parties are strong, governments with leftist and rightist tendencies will probably alternate, but if the Center is weak, the disaffected components of a coalition government may turn to their neighbors on the other side and attempt to form a rightist or leftist government.

In both two-party and multiparty systems majorities are normally obtained by a coalition of Right-and-Center or of Left-and-Center elements. Such coalitions are normal in the sense that they do not threaten the constitutional structure, and the Center, broadly viewed, is committed to the continuation of that structure.[12] So long as neither the Left nor the Right can govern without the Center, each will also be committed to the maintenance of constitutional structure. Long ago Aristotle proclaimed "that the best political community is formed by citizens of the middle class, and that those states are likely to be well-administered, in which the middle class is large, and stronger if possible than both the other classes, or at any rate than either singly; for the addition of the middle class turns the scale and prevents either of the extremes from being dominant."[13]

Such a situation is a triad of Type 5 or Type 6, with the moderates as *A,* confident of dominating the situation alone or else by means of a coalition with either radicals or reactionaries.

In the absence of a strong Center, parliamentary government is precarious, for any majority coalition will be in constant danger of domination by its extremist components. But when extremists do achieve power they are greatly tempted to consolidate it by overthrowing the parlia-

---

[12] "The term 'centre,'" says Duverger, "is applied to the geometrical spot at which the moderates of opposed tendencies meet: moderates of the Right and moderates of the Left. Every Centre is divided against itself and remains separated into two halves, Left-Centre and Right-Centre"—*op. cit.,* p. 215.

[13] Aristotle, *Politics* (New York: Modern Library, Inc., 1943), pp. 191–92.

mentary system, and even if they resist the temptation the extremists of the other wing may feel sufficiently threatened to withdraw from the system and attempt to seize power directly.

The parties of the Center represent the professionals and white-collar workers, the secure functionaries, the men of small property, and the factory workers with accumulated savings. When these are few in numbers, as in some of the new African states, parliamentary democracy will probably not survive except as an empty form. When parties of the Center are a little more numerous but are still incapable of constituting a majority, as in most of the Latin American nations, the instability of parliamentary government is stabilized, so to speak, for armed seizures of power alternate with free elections, and intervals of dictatorship with parliamentary government. Parliamentary government is subject to sudden collapse when confidence in the Center is greatly weakened by military or financial disaster. If middle-class dissatisfaction becomes sufficiently acute, there is a rapid shift of strength from the Center towards both extremes until only the choice between one coup d'état and another remains.

NONPARLIAMENTARY GOVERNMENT

National politics involve another fundamental triad composed of the government, the army, and the populace. So long as a parliamentary system is secure both the army and the populace obey the government unthinkingly and its monopoly of violence is never questioned. As soon as a seizure of power is threatened by the Left or the Right or both, the army becomes a political force, often the strongest political force.[14]

Conventional armies have a rightist inclination: their institutions are traditional and their values include authority, obedience, ritual, privilege, and adherence to archaic customs, which give them an unmistakable right-wing affinity that is often reinforced by the recruitment of officers from conservative backgrounds and the exclusion of soldiers with leftist affiliations. However, modern history is full of notable exceptions, like the Imperial regiments that supported the Bolsheviks in 1917. Many revolutionary leaders, from Cromwell to Fidel Castro, have organized new armies of their own with mixed cadres of experienced soldiers and militant revolutionists.

14 In five of the six modern coups d'état analyzed by Goodspeed (Belgrade, 1903, Petrograd, 1917, Berlin, 1920, Rome, 1922, and Rastenburg, 1944) the inclination of the army seems to have settled the outcome. In the sixth case (Dublin, 1916) the position of the army was never in doubt and the position of the rebels was therefore apparently hopeless from the start. See D. J. Goodspeed, *The Conspirators: A Study of the Coup d'État* (New York: The Viking Press, Inc., 1961).

The support the army brings to the right wing when a parliamentary system begins to crumble is often countered by the conversion of the populace into a street mob. This process seems never to be spontaneous: at times it represents the mobilization of well-disciplined unions or political societies, but more often it is brought about by coordinated agitation. In either case, the size and strength of the mob grows in the course of successive demonstrations that challenge the government to a test of strength. The sequence of events is almost invariable: first the government attempts to control the mob with its own forces of policemen and guards and if these measures are unsuccessful and the demonstrations continue, the nearest units of the army are called in for help. If the army refuses or fails to suppress the demonstrations, the government falls and is replaced by a coalition of army officers and the organizers of the mob. The new regime will survive only if it succeeds in converting or reorganizing the rest of the army very quickly.

If the army succeeds in dispersing the mob, its officers have a choice between returning peaceably to their barracks or seizing power. Which option they elect seems to depend on local customs. In countries where the army is traditionally active in politics, they are likely to form a junta and proceed to overthrow the government on their own account.

Even when parliamentary institutions have been extinguished and replaced by a rightist or leftist dictatorship, the formation of coalitions in the triad of government, army, and populace continues to determine whether a regime survives.

The principal alternative to representative government in the modern world is the one-party state. Office-holders are chosen by the inner circle of the single party. If popular elections are held, their purpose is to demonstrate the popularity of the regime, not to choose between opposing viewpoints. The power of the ruler or ruling committee is not checked by overt opposition. The constitutional safeguards that usually exist on paper are meaningless because there is no one capable of enforcing them against the government. The government is indistinguishable from the leadership of the party.

The conditions for a stable one-party system appear to be, first, the extermination or neutralization of the party's natural opponents, for example, landlords or labor leaders; second, the development of a passionate doctrine, and third, the training of an indoctrinated militia. A military regime is likely to be of brief duration unless it is reinforced by a civilian party with its own ideology.

Governing by means of street mobs is an uneasy business. Although the populace may play a crucial part in the revolution that brings about a one-party system, only a coalition of government and army (or party and army) against the populace can maintain a one-party regime. Once that coalition is established it can become nearly independent of the fluctuations of public opinion. Communist regimes in countries where much of the populace is disaffected seem quite as stable as those in countries where they enjoy widespread popular support.

When a single ruling party has developed large, well-disciplined forces and has linked them closely to the army, it may continue in power undisturbed for a very long time and its history may even be rather uneventful, like that of the Salazar dictatorship in Portugal. In the long run, however, single-party regimes are relatively unstable, for they are threatened not only by external enemies but also by factions within the ruling party and by the difficulty of arranging an orderly succession of leaders.

Neither of these problems is fortuitous. Whenever there are significant decisions to be made, differences of opinion develop among the decision-makers and thus the development of factions is inevitable under any conceivable government. One difference leads to another until the decision-makers begin to align into groups wishing to reform the existing structure, to maintain it as is, or to return it to a previous condition. Conservative, moderate, and liberal positions begin to define themselves under the umbrella of unanimity. But in the single-party state, opposition to the party line is treason, and the potential leaders of an opposition must be swiftly silenced. When differences of opinion do develop, the struggle over policy is extraordinarily bitter because it is understood that the faction which succeeds in promulgating its viewpoint as official doctrine will be entitled to remove from office or even kill its opponents. Almost every Bolshevik who played a major part in the 1917 revolution fell victim to the Soviet state in the following two decades, and the doctrinal disputes of the Chinese People's Republic have approached the scale of civil war.

Each succession to the top position in a single-party state imperils the ruling coalition. Mechanically a succession is difficult to arrange because the traditional devices—like dynastic inheritance, designation of a coadjutor, popular election, and election by a conclave are inappropriate. The successful candidate must improvise his own mode of election when the opportunity occurs and even then he may not be universally acceptable. From Richard Cromwell on, the heirs of founding dictators have often found themselves unable to maintain their positions. No matter how much interpenetration has taken place between the party and the army, the army is likely to develop a spontaneous preference for military leadership, while the party insists on a predominantly civilian government.

PATTERNS OF REVOLUTION

A triadic theory of revolution was first proposed about forty years ago by Edwards, who compared the four classic revolutions of modern times

—English, American, French, and Russian—and found many parallels among them, along with some intractable differences.[15] These four revolutions stand somewhat apart from other political upheavals that have occurred since the Renaissance because of the sweeping changes they brought to their countries and the influence they had on other countries which copied or avoided them. The similarities of detail are striking. In all four cases cited, the revolution began with a violent demonstration that the old regime was unable to control,[16] followed by the creation of an armed militia, the spontaneous appearance of new forms of local representation, the calling of a National Assembly, a period of optimism and constitutional reform presided over by moderates, a flight of conservatives into exile, intervention by foreign armies incited by these same conservatives, the raising of a mass revolutionary army to repel the invaders, a coup d'état by the radicals overthrowing the moderate regime (this took a very mild form in the American Revolution), a reign of terror followed by a reaction against the terrorists, and ultimately a dictatorship with the restoration of some features of the old regime and the return of some of the exiles.

The classic revolution begins with three main factions that Edwards calls the conservatives, the moderate-reformers, and the radicals. At the outbreak of the revolution they form a triad of Type 5. The conservatives are the strongest faction. They still control the machinery of government and can count on the support of foreign allies. But when they are taught by dramatic events like the storming of the Bastille that they can no longer rule alone, they attempt to preserve their regime by forming a coalition with the moderate-reformers and pledging themselves to a program of reform. If this program is successful, the revolution never occurs. In the classic sequence, the moderate-reformers soon repudiate their coalition with the conservatives and turn to the radicals, who are fewer in number but better organized.

The ensuing coalition of moderate-reformers and radicals sets the revolution in motion. This coalition is formed as soon as it has any chance of dominating the conservatives, and indeed, it often forms prematurely, for most attempted revolutions are abortive. Even in a successful revolution the coalition of moderate-reformers and radicals finds itself in a

---

[15] Lyford P. Edwards, *A Natural History of Revolution* (Chicago: University of Chicago Press, 1927). The later work of Brinton builds solidly on Edwards' essay and should be read as a companion volume. See Crane Brinton, *The Anatomy of Revolution* (New York: Vintage Books, Inc., 1957) (orig. pub. 1938). Edwards made a passing attempt to fit two great religious revolutions—the spread of Christianity in the Roman Empire and the Protestant Reformation—into the same pattern. Brinton confined himself to the four revolutions listed above.

[16] The defense of the five members of Parliament against King Charles' warrant by the London mob, the storming of the Bastille, the Boston Tea Party, and the February Riots in Petrograd.

precarious situation after its seizure of power. The conservatives set about regrouping their forces, and the coalition's slight advantage of power is not enough for it to govern effectively. At the same time the price of failure has been greatly increased, for the revolutionary leaders expect to be treated as traitors should the conservatives regain control.

The next step taken by the coalition of moderate-reformers and radicals is to reduce the power of the conservatives by imprisoning their leaders, depriving them of political rights, confiscating their property, and encouraging them to leave the country. Even in the American Revolution, which is the mildest example of the classic sequence, the Tories were treated in this fashion after the Declaration of Independence. What Edwards calls the "merciless despotism of the triumphant majority" [17] arouses bitter resentment among the persecuted conservatives, and some who flee the country go to their conservative allies abroad and persuade them to intervene with military forces to restore order.

In every example of the classic sequence, the success of the conservatives in provoking foreign intervention solidified the revolutionary coalition, legitimized its rule, and enabled it to make a clean sweep of the *ancien régime*. In every case, too, the military defense of the new regime was organized by men of the radical faction who emerged from the conflict with the means to dominate the moderate-reformers.

The conservatives being eliminated, two parties remain in the revolutionary state: the moderate-reformers and the radicals. Using the continued threat of foreign intervention as a pretext, the radicals institute a reign of terror with the double purpose of eliminating the moderate-reformers as a political force and repressing the conservative sentiments still held by large segments of the populace.

The next stage of the classic sequence is the "Thermidorian reaction": the reign of terror is officially terminated, its excesses are recognized, and some of those who managed it are punished in turn. The radicals are in full control, but the nation is weary of politics and is badly in need of reconstruction. There is a hurried return to normality while the surviving revolutionary leaders attempt to improvise a stable form of government.[18]

At this point the courses of the several classic revolutions diverged.

[17] Edwards, *op. cit.*, p. 121.

[18] The similarities among the four revolutions are due in part to deliberate imitation. The leaders of the American Revolution were exceedingly familiar with the history of England during the Commonwealth, the French Revolution drew on the ideology of both its predecessors, and Lenin was a specialist in the history of revolutions who also made a careful study of all the subversive movements in Russian history, which had been numerous and violent. See R. H. Bruce Lockhart, *The Two Revolutions* (Chester Springs, Pa.: Dufour Editions, 1967). The two recent revolutions that seem to follow the classic sequence—the Chinese and the Cuban—have both been conducted by men familiar with the theory that revolutions follow a natural course but who have consciously determined to modify that course at various points.

Cromwell's dictatorship took on the semblance of a constitutional monarchy and paved the way for the restoration of the Stuarts, Washington's military dictatorship gave way to a weak and unstable congressional government. The Thermidorian period in France led unexpectedly to the Directory and the First Empire, and the Thermidorian reactions in Russia—and in China and Cuba—were nipped in the bud. In each of these cases the leader of the revolution was able to establish himself as a semidivine hero ruling in the name of the triumphant masses. In the English, American, and French revolutions, a new faction of conservatives appeared during the Thermidorian reaction and soon made common cause with the returned exiles and the underground survivors of the old regime. In the Russian, Chinese, and Cuban revolutions, the conservatives were totally destroyed as a political force and the moderate-reformers lost their identity. The terrible struggles that later shook these one-party states involved two factions distinguishable only as pro-dictator and anti-dictator. Most of the veterans of the revolution whose claims to influence were not based on the favor of the dictator, found themselves, voluntarily or not, in the anti-dictator faction and were eventually eliminated.

GLOSSARY

A *social system* is a system whose elements are persons or groups of persons, and whose relationships are established by social interaction.

A *triad* is a social system containing three interrelated actors.

A *coalition* is a combination of two or more actors who adopt a common strategy in contention with other actors in the same system.

A *coalition in a triad* is a combination of two members of the triad directed against the third member.

Power is the ability of an actor to modify the behavior of other actors with whom he interacts.

An actor is said to *dominate* another in a particular situation, when his power over the other is clearly greater than the other's power over him.

The *power distribution* of a triad is a description or measurement of the relative power of each member at a given time.

The formation of a coalition in a triad divides the triad into two *partners* and one *opponent*.

In *continuous situations* involving triads, the formation and dissolution of coalitions is an informal, spontaneous, and irregular process.

In *episodic situations* involving triads, coalition formation occurs at predictable intervals under stated rules.

In *terminal situations* involving triads, coalitions are formed for the purpose of eliminating the opponent from the triad.

The *solidarity* of a coalition is its ability to resist the formation of alternative coalition.

A *winning coalition* is a coalition that dominates its opponent.

The *cheapest winning coalition* in a triad is the coalition that dominates its opponent by a lesser margin than any other winning coalition.

The *equitable expectation* is that coalition partners will demand shares of any payoff to the coalition that are roughly proportional to their contribution of resources to the coalition.

An *organization* is a social system that has an unequivocal collective identity, an exact roster of members, an explicit program of activity, and procedures for replacing members.

A *status schism* is the division of a set of organizational positions into higher and lower categories, between which coalitions are prohibited.

An *organizational triad* is a triad whose members belong to an organization and are required by its program to interact with one another.

The *superior member* of an organizational triad is the member with the highest organizational status.

The *official program* of an organizational triad is the schedule of goal-directed activity prescribed for its members by the organization.

The *private programs* of an organizational triad are the schedules of goal-directed activity established by its members in pursuit of their own interests.

A *conservative coalition* in an organizational triad is a coalition that does not upset the prescribed status order.

A *revolutionary coalition* in an organizational triad is a coalition that dominates the superior member of the triad.

An *improper coalition* in an organizational triad is a coalition that is neither conservative nor revolutionary.

Triads are *linked* when they have one or two members in common.

When the superior member of one triad is a middle or inferior member of a linked triad, the latter is called the *superior triad*.

BIBLIOGRAPHY ON COALITIONS IN TRIADS

Anderson, Robert C., "A Sociometric Approach to the Analysis of Inter-organizational Relationships," Institute for Community Development, Continuing Education Service, Michigan State University (August 1967).

Apple, Dorrian, "The Social Structure of Grandparenthood," *American Anthropologist,* LVIII (August 1956), 656–63.

Arensberg, Conrad, and Kimball, Solon T., *Family and Community in Ireland* (Cambridge, Mass.: Harvard University Press, 1940).

Aristotle, *Politics* (New York: Modern Library, Inc., 1943).

Barth, Fredrik, "Segmentary Opposition and the Theory of Games: A Study of Pathan Organization," *Journal of the Royal Anthropological Institute,* LXXXIX (1959), 5–21.

Bartos, Otomar J., "How Predictable Are Negotiations?", *Journal of Conflict Resolution,* XI, No. 4 (December 1967), 481–96.

Berkowitz, Leonard, Levy, Bernard I., and Harvey, Arthur R., "Effects of Performance Evaluation on Group Integration and Motivation," *Human Relations,* X (1957), 195–208.

Blood, Robert O., Jr., and Wolfe, Donald L., *Husbands and Wives: The Dynamics of Married Living* (New York: Glencoe Press, 1960).

Bond, John R., and Vinacke, W. Edgar, "Coalitions in Mixed Sex Triads," *Sociometry*, XXIV, No. 1 (March 1961), 61–75.

Boote, Alfred S., "A Study of Triadic Living Groups in a College Dormitory," unpublished manuscript, Stanford University, Department of Sociology, 1957.

Borgatta, Marie L., "Power Structure and Coalitions in Three-Person Groups," *Journal of Social Psychology*, LV (December 1961), 287–300.

Bott, Elizabeth, *Family and Social Network: Roles, Norms, and External Relationships in Ordinary Urban Families* (London: Tavistock Publications, 1957).

Bowerman, Charles E., and Elder, Glen H., Jr., "Variations in Adolescent Perception of Family Power Structure," *American Sociological Review*, XXIX, No. 4 (August 1964), 551–67.

Brant, C. S., "On Joking Relationships," *American Anthropologist*, L, No. 1 (January 1948), 160–62.

Brinton, Crane, *The Anatomy of Revolution* (New York: Vintage Books, Inc., 1957). Orig. pub. 1938.

Bronfenbrenner, Uri, "Some Familial Antecedents of Responsibility and Leadership in Adolescence," in Luigi Petrullo and Bernard M. Bass, eds., *Leadership and Interpersonal Behavior* (New York: Holt, Rinehart & Winston, Inc., 1961), 239–71.

Campbell, Donald T., "The Mutual Methodological Relevance of Anthropology and Sociology," in Francis L. K. Hsu, ed., *Psychological Anthropology* (Homewood, Ill.: Richard D. Irwin, Inc., 1961).

Cancian, Francesca, "Interaction Patterns in Zinacanteco Families," *American Sociological Review*, XXIX, No. 4 (August 1964), 540–50.

Caplow, Theodore, "Further Development of a Theory of Coalitions in the Triad," *American Journal of Sociology*, XLIV (March 1959), 488–93.

———, "A Theory of Coalitions in the Triad," *American Sociological Review*, XXI, No. 4 (August 1956), 489–93.

———, *Principles of Organization* (New York: Harcourt, Brace & World, Inc., 1964).

Chaney, Marilyn V., and Vinacke, W. Edgar, "Achievement and Nurturance in Triads Varying in Power Distribution," *Journal of Abnormal and Social Psychology*, LX, No. 2 (March 1960), 176–81.

Chapman, Loren J., and Campbell, Donald T., "An Attempt to Predict the Performance of Three-Man Teams from Attitude Measures," *Journal of Social Psychology*, XLVI (1957), 277–86.

Coleman, James, "The Use of Electronic Computers in the Study of Social Organization," *Archives of European Sociology,* VI (1965), 89–107.

Coser, Lewis, ed., *Georg Simmel* (Englewood Cliffs, N.J.: Prentice-Hall, Inc., 1965).

Crozier, Michel, *The Bureaucratic Phenomenon* (Chicago: University of Chicago Press, 1964).

Davis, James A., and Leinhardt, Samuel, "The Structure of Positive Interpersonal Relations in Small Groups," Dartmouth College, 1967 (mimeographed).

Davis, Kingsley, "Intermarriage in Caste Societies," in Rose Laub Coser, ed., *The Family: Its Structure and Functions* (New York: St. Martin's Press, Inc., 1964).

Devereux, Edward C., Bronfenbrenner, Uri, and Susi, George J., "Patterns of Parents; Behavior in the United States of America and the Federal Republic of Germany: A Cross-National Comparison," *International Social Science Journal,* XIV (1962), 488–506.

DeVore, Irven, ed., *Primate Behavior* (New York: Holt, Rinehart & Winston, Inc., 1965).

Duverger, Maurice, *Political Parties* (2nd ed.) (London: Methuen & Co., Ltd., 1961).

Edwards, Lyford P., *A Natural History of Revolution* (Chicago: University of Chicago Press, 1927).

Elder, Glen H., Jr., "Family Structure and Educational Attainment: A Cross-National Analysis," *American Sociological Review,* XXX, No. 1 (February 1965), 81–96.

Evans-Pritchard, E. E., *Kinship and Marriage Among the Nuer* (Oxford: Clarendon Press, 1951).

Firth, Raymond, *We the Tikopia: A Sociological Study of Kinship in Primitive Polynesia* (Boston: Beacon Press, 1963). Orig. pub. 1936.

Freilich, Morris, "The Natural Triad in Kinship and Complex Systems," *American Sociological Review,* XXIX, No. 4 (August 1964), 529–40.

Gamson, William A., "An Experimental Test of a Theory of Coalition Formation," *American Sociological Review,* XXVI, No. 4 (August 1961), 565–73.

————, "A Theory of Coalition Formation," *American Sociological Review,* XXVI, No. 3 (June 1961), 373–82.

Geis, Florence L., "Machiavellianism and the Manipulation of One's Fellow Man," Ph.D. dissertation, Columbia University, Department of Social Psychology, 1964.

Gerstl, Joel, *Coalitions in Sibling Triads,* University of Minnesota, Department of Sociology, 1956 (mimeographed).

Goodspeed, D. J., *The Conspirators: A Study of the Coup d'État* (New York: The Viking Press, Inc., 1961).

Gough, E. Kathleen, "The Nayars and the Definition of Marriage," *Journal of the Royal Anthropological Institute,* LXXXIX (1959), 23–34.

Haley, Jay, "The Family of the Schizophrenic: A Model System," in Gerald Handel, ed., *The Psychosocial Interior of the Family: A Sourcebook for the Study of Whole Families* (Chicago: Aldine Publishing Company, 1967).

Heider, Fritz, "Attitudes and Cognitive Organization," *Journal of Psychology,* XXI (January 1946), 107–12.

———, *The Psychology of Interpersonal Relations* (New York: John Wiley & Sons, Inc., 1958).

Heisse, George A., and Miller, George A., "Problem Solving by Small Groups Using Various Communication Nets," *Journal of Abnormal and Social Psychology,* XLVI (1951), 327–36.

Herbst, P. G., "Conceptual Framework for Studying the Family," in Oscar A. Oeser, and S. B. Hammond, eds., *Social Structure and Personality in a City* (London: Routledge & Kegan Paul Ltd., 1954), 126–37.

Hirschman, A. O., "Models of Reformmongering," in his *Journeys Toward Progress* (New York: The Twentieth Century Fund, 1963), pp. 276–97.

Hoffman, Paul H., *et al.,* "Tendencies Toward Group Comparability in Competitive Bargaining," *Human Relations,* VII (1954), 141–59.

Hsu, Francis L. K., "Kinship and Ways of Life: An Exploration," in *Psychological Anthropology: Approaches to Culture and Personality* (Homewood, Ill.: Richard D. Irwin, Inc., 1961).

Iklé, Fred Charles, *How Nations Negotiate* (New York: Harper & Row, Publishers, 1964).

Irish, Donald P., "Sibling Interaction: A Neglected Aspect in Family Life Research," in Bernard Farber, ed., *Kinship and Family Organization* (New York: John Wiley & Sons, Inc., 1966), 149–58.

Kaplan, Morton A., "Balance of Power, Bipolar and Other Models of International Systems," *American Political Science Review,* LI (1957), 684–95. ·

————, Burns, Arthur, and Quandt, Richard, "Theoretical Analysis of 'Balance of Power,'" *Behavioral Science,* V, No. 3 (1960), 240–52.

Karlsson, George, "Some Aspects of Power in Small Groups," in Joan H. Criswell, *et al.,* eds., *Mathematical Methods in Small Group Processes* (Stanford, Calif.: Stanford University Press, 1962), 193–202.

Kelley, Harold H., and Arrowood, A. John, "Coalitions in the Triad: Critique and Experiment," *Sociometry,* XXIII, No. 3 (September 1960), 231–44.

Kirkpatrick, Clifford, *The Family as Process and Institution* (2nd ed.) (New York: The Ronald Press Company, 1963).

Kohn, Melvin L., and Clausen, John, "Parental Authority Behavior and Schizophrenia," *American Journal of Ortho-Psychiatry,* XXVI (April 1956), 297–313.

Lennard, Henry L., Epstein, Leon J., and Katzung, Bertram G., "Psychoactive Drug Action and Group Interaction Process," *The Journal of Nervous and Mental Disease,* CVL, No. 1 (1967), 69–78.

Lieberman, Bernhardt, "Experimental Studies of Conflict in Some Two-Person and Three-Person Games," in Joan H. Criswell, *et al., Mathematical Methods in Small Group Processes* (Stanford, Calif.: Stanford University Press), 203–20.

————, "*i*-Trust: A Notion of Trust in Three-Person Games and International Affairs," *Journal of Conflict Resolution,* VIII (1964), 271–80.

Lidz, Theodore; Parker, Beula, and Cornelison, Alice, "The Role of the Father in the Family Environment of the Schizophrenic Patient," *American Journal of Psychiatry,* CXIII (1956), 126–32.

Liska, George, *International Equilibrium* (Cambridge, Mass.: Harvard University Press, 1967).

Lockhart, R. H. Bruce, *The Two Revolutions* (Chester Springs, Pa.: Dufour Editions, 1967).

Luce, R. Duncan, and Rogow, Arnold A., "A Game Theoretical Analysis of Congressional Power Distributions for a Stable Two-Party System," *Behavioral Science,* I, No. 2 (April 1956), 83–95.

McGrath, Joseph E., "A Social Psychological Approach to the Study of Negotiation," in Raymond V. Bowers, ed., *Studies on Behavior in Organizations: A Research Symposium* (Athens, Ga.: University of Georgia Press, 1966), 101–34.

Malinowski, Bronislaw, *The Father in Primitive Psychology* (New York: W. W. Norton & Company, Inc., 1927).

Mason, William A., "The Effects of Environmental Restriction on the Social Development of Rhesus Monkeys," in Charles H. Southwick, ed., *Primate Social Behavior* (Princeton, N.J.: D. Van Nostrand Co., Inc., 1963), 161–73.

Meyerson, Martin, and Banfield, Edward C., *Politics, Planning, and the Public Interest: The Case of Public Housing in Chicago* (New York: Glencoe Press, 1955).

Mills, Theodore M., "The Coalition Pattern in Three-Person Groups," *American Sociological Review*, XIX, No. 6 (December 1964).

———, "Development Processes in Three-Person Groups," *Human Relations*, IX, No. 3 (1956).

———, et al., *Group Structure and the Newcomer: An Experimental Study of Group Expansion* (Oslo, Norway: Oslo University Press, 1957).

———, "Power Relations in Three-Person Groups," *American Sociological Review*, XVIII, No. 4 (August 1953), 351–57.

Morgan, William R., and Sawyer, Jack, "Bargaining, Expectations, and the Preference for Equality Over Equity," *Journal of Personality and Social Psychology*, VI, No. 2 (1967), 139–49.

Morris, Desmond, *The Naked Ape: A Zoologist's Study of the Human Animal* (London: Jonathan Cape Limited, 1967).

Morrisette, Julian O.; Jahnke, John C., and Baker, Keith, "Structural Balance: A Test of the Completeness Hypothesis," *Behavioral Science*, XI, No. 2 (March 1966), 121–25.

Murdock, George Peter, *Social Structure* (New York: The Macmillan Company, 1949).

Nadel, S. F., *The Theory of Social Structure* (New York: Glencoe Press, 1964), esp. Chap. 5, "Degrees of Abstraction."

Newcomb, Theodore M., *The Acquaintance Process* (New York: Holt, Rinehart & Winston, Inc., 1961).

O'Rourke, John F., "Field and Laboratory: The Decision-Making Behavior of Family Groups in Two Experimental Conditions," *Sociometry*, XXVI, No. 4 (December 1963), 422–35.

Parsons, Talcott, and Bales, Robert F., *Family, Socialization and Interaction Process* (New York: Glencoe Press, 1955).

Pitts, Jesse, "The Case of the French Bourgeoisie," in Rose Laub Coser, ed., *The Family: Its Structure and Functions* (New York: St. Martin's Press, Inc., 1954), 545–50.

Poitou, Jean-Pierre, "Perception des contributions individuelles au travail de groupe dans une structure social hierarchisée," *Psychologie Française*, IX, No. 4 (1964), 304–15.

Priest, Robert F., and Sawyer, Jack, "Proximity and Peership: Bases of Balance in Interpersonal Attraction," *American Journal of Sociology,* LXXII, No. 6 (May 1967), 633–49.

Radcliffe-Brown, A. R., "On Joking Relationships," *Africa,* XIII (1940), 195–210.

———, *Structure and Function in Primitive Society* (London: Cohen & West, Ltd., 1952).

———, "The Study of Kinship Systems," *Journal of the Royal Anthropological Institute,* LXXI (1941), 1–18.

Rainwater, Lee, "Crucible of Identity: The Negro Lower-Class Family," *Daedalus,* XCV (1966), 172–216.

Riker, William H., *The Theory of Political Coalitions* (New Haven: Yale University Press, 1962).

Rosen, Bernard C., "Socialization and Achievement Motivation in Brazil," *American Sociological Review,* XXVII, No. 5 (October 1962), 612–24.

Rosenthal, Howard, *Simulating Elections in Western Democracies,* Carnegie Institute of Technology, 1967 (mimeographed).

Roy, Donald, "Efficiency and 'the Fix': Informal Intergroup Relations in a Piecework Machine Shop," *American Journal of Sociology,* LX, No. 3 (November 1954), 255–66.

St. Ehrlich, Vera, *Family in Transition: A Study of 300 Yugoslav Villages* (Princeton, N.J.: Princeton University Press, 1966).

Sawyer, Jack, and Guetzkow, Harold, "Bargaining and Negotiation in International Relations," Chap. 13 in Herbert C. Kelman, ed., *International Behavior: A Social-Psychological Analysis* (New York: Holt, Rinehart and Winston, Inc., 1965).

Schapera, I., *Married Life in an African Tribe* (Evanston, Ill.: Northwestern University Press, 1966).

Schlien, John M., "Mother-in-law, A Problem in Kinship Terminology," in Hyman Rodman, ed., *Marriage, Family and Society* (New York: Random House, Inc., 1965).

Simmel, Georg, "How is Society Possible?", in Kurt H. Wolff, trans. and ed., *Georg Simmel, 1858–1918* (Columbus: Ohio State University Press, 1959), 337–56.

———, "The Number of Members as Determining the Sociological Form of the Group," *American Journal of Sociology,* VIII, No. 1 (July 1902), 1–46 and 158–96.

———, *The Sociology of Georg Simmel,* Kurt H. Wolff, trans., ed., and introd. (New York: Glencoe Press, 1950).

————, *Conflict*, Kurt H. Wolff, trans., and *The Web of Group Affilia-tions*, Reinhard Bendix, trans. (New York: Glencoe Press, 1955).

Slater, Philip, "Parental Role Differentiation," *American Journal of Sociology*, XLVII, No. 3 (November 1961), 296–311.

Sprott, W. J. H., *Human Groups* (Baltimore: Penguin Books, Inc., 1958).

Spykman, Nicholas J., *The Social Theory of Georg Simmel* (New York: Atherton Press, 1966).

Strodtbeck, Fred L., "The Family as a Three-Person Group," *American Sociological Review*, XIX (1954), 23–29.

Stryker, Sheldon, and Psathas, George, "Research on Coalitions in the Triad: Findings, Problems, and Strategy," *Sociometry*, XXIII, No. 3 (September 1960), 217–30.

Sussman, Marvin B., and Burchinal, Lee G., "Kin Family Network: Un-heralded Structure in Current Conceptualizations of Family Func-tioning," in Bernard Farber, ed., *Kinship and Family Organization* (New York: John Wiley & Sons, Inc., 1966), 123–33.

Torrance, Paul Ed., "Some Consequences of Power Differences on Deci-sion-Making in Permanent and Temporary Three-Man Groups," in A. Paul Hare, Edgar F. Borgatta, and Robert F. Bales, eds., *Small Groups: Studies in Social Interaction* (revised ed.) (New York: Alfred A. Knopf, Inc., 1965).

Tunstall, Jeremy, *The Advertising Man in London Advertising Agencies* (London: Chapman & Hall Ltd., 1964).

Turk, Theresa (University of North Carolina), and Turk, Herman (Duke University), "Group Interaction in a Formal Setting: The Case of the Triad," unpublished paper, 1961.

Turner, Ralph H., "Some Aspects of Women's Ambition," *American Journal of Sociology*, LXX, No. 3 (November 1964).

Uesugi, Thomas K., and Vinacke, W. Edgar, "Strategy in a Feminine Game," *Sociometry*, XXVI, No. 1 (March 1963), 75–88.

Vinacke, W. Edgar, "The Effects of Cumulative Score on Coalition For-mation in Triads with Various Patterns of Internal Power," *Amer-ican Psychologist*, XIV (July 1959), 381.

————, *Foundations of Psychology* (New York: American Book Com-pany, 1968).

————, "Puissance, stratégie et formation de coalitions dans les triades dans quatre conditions experimentales," *Bulletin du C. E. R. P.*, XIII, No. 3 (1964), 119–44.

————, "Sex Roles in a Three Person Game," *Sociometry*, XXII, No. 4 (December 1959), 343–60.

————, and Arkoff, Abe, "An Experimental Study of Coalitions in the Triad," *American Sociological Review,* XXII, No. 4 (August 1957), 406–14.

von Clausewitz, Karl, *War, Politics and Power,* E. M. Collins, ed. and trans. (Chicago: Henry Regnery Co., 1962).

von Neumann, John, and Morgenstern, Oskar, *Theory of Games and Economic Behavior* (Princeton, N. J.: Princeton University Press, 1954).

von Wiese, Leopold, and Becker, Howard, *Systematic Sociology* (New York: John Wiley & Sons, Inc., 1932).

Walton, Richard E., *Third Party Roles in Interdepartmental Conflict,* Purdue University, Institute for Research in the Behavioral, Economic and Management Sciences, Paper #184, 1967.

Williams, Thomas Rhys, *The Dusun: A North Borneo Society* (New York: Holt, Rinehart & Winston, Inc., 1965).

Willems, Emilio, "The Structure of the Brazilian Family," *Social Forces,* XXXI (May 1953).

Willerman, Ben, "A Final Report: Research on Cohesive and Disruptive Tendencies in Coalition-Type Groups," University of Minnesota, 1957 (mimeographed).

Willis, Richard H., "Coalitions in the Tetrad," *Sociometry,* XXV, No. 4 (December 1962), 358–76.

Wright, Quincy, *A Study of War* (2nd. ed.) (Chicago: University of Chicago Press, 1965).

Zelditch, Morris, Jr., "Role Differentiation in the Nuclear Family: A Comparative Study," in Norman W. Bell and Ezra F. Vogel, *A Modern Introduction to the Family* (New York: Glencoe Press, 1960), 329–38.

INDEX